Real World 101

A Survival Guide to Life After High School

Autumn McAlpin

Sourced Media Books
San Clemente, California

For Brandon—
and impossible without the loving support of Michael.

Published by
Sourced Media Books
20 Via Cristobal, San Clemente, CA 92673 U.S.A.
www.sourcedmedia.net

ISBN: 1-4392-3983-5

Printed in the United States of America.

This publication is designed to provide accurate and authoritative information with regard to the subject matter covered. It is sold with the understanding that the publisher is not engaged in rendering legal, accounting, or other professional advice. If legal advice or other expert assistance
is required, the services of a competent profesional person should be
sought.
—From a *Declaration of Principles* jointly adopted by a
Committee of the American Bar Association and a
Committee of Publishers and Associations

Many of the designations used by manufacurers and sellers to distinguish
their products are claimed as trademarks. Where those designations appear in this book and Sourced Media Books was aware of a trademark
claim, the designations have been printed with initial capital letters.

Contents

Introduction vi

Part 1: Surviving College 1

Chapter 1: From Applications to Acceptance:
The Inside Scoop on College 3

Chapter 2: The Four-Year Plan:
How to Plan Your Class Schedule So You
Can Actually Graduate by Twenty-One 15

Chapter 3: Schmoozing Your Way to an "A":
How to Convince Your Professor You're an
"A" Student—Even If You're Not 29

Chapter 4: Writing Tips Even "-ology"
Majors Need to Know 37

Chapter 5: Hitting the Books
(in a Nonviolent Way) 51

Chapter 6: Justifying Socializing as Social Work:
Ways to Build a Good Resume 61

Part 2: Surviving Your First Home Away
from Home 71

Chapter 7: Playing House 73

Chapter 8: Windex, Pledge, and Other Strange
Bottles You'll Find Under the Sink 85

Chapter 9: Get Your Security Deposit Back:
How to Handle Basic Home Repairs 95

Chapter 10: How to Keep Bleeding and Shrinking
Out of the Laundromat 103

Chapter 11: Getting "Customer Service,
May I Help You?" to Help You 109

Chapter 12: On the Road Again. 117

Part 3: Surviving Financially 129

Chapter 13: How to Get, Keep, and Quit a Job 131

Chapter 14: From the Bank to the Balance Book:
How to Set Up, Balance, and Build Your Account 143

Chapter 15: The Seven-Year Mistake:
Understanding Credit 157

Chapter 16: Pay Now . . . Or Pay Later:
Understanding Insurance. 167

Chapter 17: Bartering, Bargaining, and
Other Ways to Annoy Salespeople 177

Chapter 18: Welcome to the World of
Budgeters and Cheapskates 183

Part 4: Surviving Physically. 197

Chapter 19: Avoiding the "Freshman Fifteen" 199

Chapter 20: Pepper Spray and the
Police Station: Protect Yourself! 209

Chapter 21: Call Mom, or Call 911?
How to Handle Aches and Pains. 217

Chapter 22: The Difference Between Barbecuing and Boiling—and Other Cooking Basics 227

Chapter 23: Where Do They Keep the Nutmeg? And What's Nutmeg? 239

Chapter 24: Making Sure You're Not the Smelly Kid. 247

Part 5: Surviving the Social Scene 255

Chapter 25: Road Trip! 257

Chapter 26: The "It" Factor: Four Steps to Small-Town Fame 265

Chapter 27: Dating Do's and Don'ts 271

Chapter 28: It's My Party, I Can Cry if I Want to! How to Host a Party Without Too Many Tears. 281

Chapter 29: The Art of Gift-Giving 293

Chapter 30: How to Truly Live 299

Acknowledgments 307

Introduction

There's a good chance someone fed you Cheerios and dressed you in OshKosh B'Gosh during your Sesame Street years. When you went to your first sleepover, Mommy packed the bag. When you had a sniffle, Daddy took you to the doctor. What a life! The problem is—you're seventeen now, and you still don't know where they keep the luggage or how to look up the doctor's phone number!

But who needs to know how to do such things with Mom and Dad around? Guess what—as you are thrust from the commencement stage into the Real World, pampering parents are a thing of the past. You're going to have to learn a few things, and you're going to want to know them fast! How do I balance a checkbook? How do I make spaghetti? How do I get the barbecue stains out of my roommate's sweater? Aaaagh!

Don't stress—I understand. I used to be just like you. After a few years of figuring things out through trial and error (and several hundred phone calls home), I've learned the basics to surviving the chaos of the Real World, and believe me, it's much more challenging than some MTV reality show.

My eighteen-year-old brother recently moved to my town to attend a local community college. Two thousand miles away, our very worried mom asked me to help him get settled. I spent a couple of hours driving him around to sign an apartment rental agreement, get groceries, set up a bank account, and do other getting-settled-type things. Because I had already been living on my own for several years, I had forgotten how difficult doing these things can be for the first time. My brother quickly reminded me. Following are the highlights of our conversation as we sat in the car outside of the bank:

Brother: What do I do?

Me: Go in and set up an account.

Brother: What do I say?

Me: That you need to set up a checking and savings account.

Brother (blank look): How much does that cost?

Me: It should be free; banks handle your money, they don't usually charge you money. Your checks might cost a fee, but you could just get an ATM card instead.

Brother: That's the same thing as a credit card, right?

Me: No, a credit card sends you a bill and an ATM card deducts money straight out of your checking account.

Brother: How much money is in my checking account?

Me (exasperated): However much money you put in it!

Brother: But, I don't have any money.

Okay, so unfortunately most high schools don't offer a class called "Real World 101." But whether you're going to college or just moving out on your own, when you leave home for the first time, there will be many basic things you will not have a clue how to do. While doting parents mean well, their "I'll take care of it" techniques somewhat hinder their children when they enter the Real World. The Real World will not care that you never learned how to change a tire on the freeway; it will just be mad at you for blocking traffic. The bank will not care that you "forgot" to reconcile your account; they will happily charge you thirty-five bucks every time you bounce a check. Your roommates will not care that you don't know the difference between laundry detergent and fabric softener; they will just want you to stop smelling up the apartment after wearing the same socks for three weeks.

This book is meant to be a guide to handling some of the basics of grown-up life. It is written by a formerly clueless girl who encountered and endured reality—without a survival guide. And here is what I learned.

part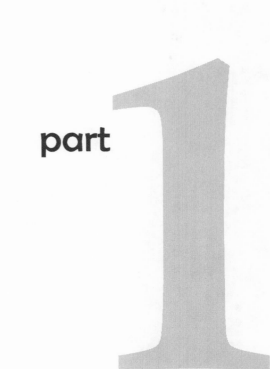

Surviving College

chapter 1

From Applications to Acceptance: The Inside Scoop on College

Which aspect of college life do you have to look forward to? Take this quiz to find out:

1. S.A.T. stands for:
   a. Surf and Turf
   b. Senior Alcoholic Testing
   c. Scholastic Aptitude Test

2. My dream dorm would be called:
   a. What's a dorm?
   b. Frat House!
   c. Little Pascals

3. My top three choices are:
   a. Wendy's, Taco Bell, and Pizza Hut
   b. Florida State, San Diego State, and University of Hawaii
   c. Pepperdine, Vanderbilt, and Duke

> **If you scored:**
> **Mostly a's:** Summer school! Summer school!
> **Mostly b's:** Sororities! Sororities!
> **Mostly c's:** Scholarship! Scholarship!

If you've already received a college acceptance letter and mailed off a tuition check, congratulations! Bravo! Good for you! You can just skim through this first section, all the while patting yourself on the back for your masterful accomplishments. But if you're like most high school seniors who don't form a "plan" until after senior trip, you may want to consign your brain to the following.

College Applications

College preparation should actually begin well before senior year. Those who know this by the third grade will graduate with honors and go Ivy League. Those of you who don't figure it out until post-puberty may enjoy summer school and tutoring sessions with the old, wrinkled, retired English teacher down the street; but don't worry, you can catch up. Since your grades and accomplishments from ninth grade on will affect your transcript and college application, don't waste time! See your guidance counselor for specific help, but following are some of the most important things you can do to be prepared, starting from the first day an upperclassman paints an "F" on your forehead.

Pick the right classes. Choose classes that are both interesting and challenging. If you are interested in what you are taking and challenged by the material, you will more likely put forth a better effort, which will result in better grades. Throw in some honors and A.P. classes, if you can pass them. Taking A.P. Biology looks much more impressive than taking seven P.E.'s. Also, make sure you are taking the kinds of classes you need to fulfill your college's acceptance requirements.

Find some extracurricular activities. Colleges look for well-rounded students, so gain a variety of hands-on experience in volunteerism, athletics, academic clubs, and the arts. While you may be your local Wii-master, colleges don't deem any activity that takes place in front of a television screen as highly beneficial to a youngster's mind. If you are looking to get into a special arts program in college or to play for the NCAA, now is also the time to find out how to fulfill those requirements.

Make a financial plan. Graduation night is way too late of a time to find out that you're going to be footing the bill for college. Talk with your family now so that you know if they will be forking out the dough, or if you'll need to start a dog-washing service this summer. You can find countless books in your local libraries or bookstores that list the different grants and loans you can apply for, or contact the government for the Free Application for Financial Aid (*www.fafsa. ed.gov*) to see if you qualify.

Take—and retake—the standardized tests. To practice taking standardized tests, you can sit in a cold, quiet room early one Saturday morning with two sharpened #2 pencils, filling in imaginary circles on sheets of paper. Or, you can take the PSAT and other practice tests (don't worry, colleges won't see these scores), or attend test-taking strategy classes. There are two basic standardized tests that colleges look at— the SAT and the ACT. Find out which one is preferred by the college you want to go to, or just go ahead and take them both for fun—if you're into that sort of thing. Remember that most people can boost their scores with each retake, so sign up again if your first score is lower than your years on earth. You will want to start taking these tests during your junior year, so check with your guidance counselor for the registration deadlines.

Start looking at colleges. Throughout high school, listen to the word-of-mouth accounts of which schools have the best lacrosse teams, business schools, and tailgate parties. Make a mental list of possible schools you would like to go to, and visit a few. Making college trips during your senior year is a good, fun way to see what a college has to offer, and most high schools will excuse your absences for such trips—as long as they're not taking place weekly. If you want to find out more about what different schools have to offer, check with your guidance counselor, college guidebooks, college fairs, catalogues, and on the Internet (every college has a website). After you have weighed all your options, make a list of the pros and cons for each school, and measure that against how well you fit into the personality of the school.

Apply to colleges. Narrow the list down to a few colleges you really would like to attend, and request applications. You can even apply to some schools online. It may cost a fee to apply, so make sure you are serious about the school and you actually have a chance at being accepted before you waste the time and money. It is a good idea to apply to the large and highly competitive universities before December of your senior year.

Don't slack off yet! Colleges will still look at the classes you take and the grades you earn during your senior year. So, don't get senioritis until you've framed your acceptance letter. Then, start planning that senior trip!

What Do Colleges Look For?

Colleges know exactly what they are looking for in the prospective student pool, and you will be judged on how clearly you meet their requirements—or on how much money Gramps has contributed to the athletic department. While some schools seem to showcase carbon copy students, most are looking for unique and diverse people. Following are the general requirements that admissions committees look for in an applicant:

- GPA: How high and consistent is it? Did it improve over the years?

- Class Selection: How difficult and advanced was your course load?

- Class rank

- ACT and/or SAT scores

- Extracurricular activities: Were you in student government, the Key Club, the band, or on the soccer team? Did you volunteer every Friday or hold leadership positions?

- Awards/Achievements: Did you receive any scholastic, extracurricular, or community recognition?

- Letters of Recommendation: How well did you know the person who wrote the recommendation, and how high is his or her opinion of you?

- Essays: Most applications require at least one essay in which you should demonstrate how creative, talented, and competent you are—in a very compliant, original, and humble way, of course. The admissions board is not just looking for a good writer, but for someone who is unique and confident. So remember all those Christmas card letters your mom wrote about the time you climbed Mount Everest? Learned origami? Built an orphanage in Mexico? Now's the chance to tell your version of the story.

"I Got In!!! Now What?"

When that glorious day arrives when you eagerly rip open the envelope and proudly hold up your long-awaited acceptance letter as sunbeams shoot down from the sky and shine on the glory that is you, enjoy the moment. Aaaaw. Now keep reading—you still have a lot of work to do.

Where Are You Going to Live?

Campus housing gets a bit tricky wherever you go. So many campuses are overcrowded that applying for housing may be harder than getting in to the school itself. "First come, first served" applies in this matter, so try to get your name on a waiting list as soon as you know where you want to live—hopefully before kindergarten.

At some universities, freshmen are required to live in dorms; but even if they're not, dorm life is usually the best option for first-year students. You will meet more people there in one year than you would in four years of off-campus living. Check out the "aura" of the dorm or housing unit you like. At the university I went to, all freshmen lived in dorms, and each dorm had a general type that lived there: the jock hall, the party hall, the rich kids' hall, the study hall, the granola hall—you get the picture. If you shop for housing by matching yourself to the personality of the house, you're bound to make a few good friends.

If you still think dorm life is not for you, visit the school far in advance to explore other housing options. Check out the rental listings on the school's advertising board, or those in the local newspaper. But never sign a rental agreement without seeing the place first, because the words people use to advertise their properties are often kind exaggerations. "Cozy" usually means "tiny"; "Charming fixer upper" actually means "Nothing works!" and "Great starter home" really means "Great! Start looking around again!"

Before you agree to any living arrangement, make sure you know what utility bills (phone, cable, electric, water) you will be responsible for paying. When you sign a contractual agreement, you will most likely be expected to pay first and/ or last month's rent as well as a security deposit that will be refunded upon move-out if you leave the place in good condition. So make sure you bring your piggy bank.

Be aware of the terms of the lease as well—specifically how long you are committed to living there and if you are allowed to sublet. I have some friends who decided, after three months of living in an apartment that had a shower and dishwasher that worked every once in a while, that they were ready to get out. Unfortunately, they were in a one-year contract. Though we had fun plotting ways to get them evicted (buy a drum set, never use "inside voices," invite the local nudist colony to swim at the pool), they realized they were stuck. So, beware.

Many students are enticed by the lures of Greek life, which exists on many college campuses. While frat houses and sorority houses recruit freshmen each year to pledge, you won't be allowed to live there until you are a full-fledged (or "pledged") member. Living in these houses will most likely be a very fun, very wild, very not study-conducive atmosphere, but if you chose a particular Greek sect for its personality, you may feel right at home!

Almost every college student will agree that where you live is not nearly as important as with whom you live. So, when you go house-hunting, bring along your future roommate, if you know who this lucky person is. If not, read on.

Picking a Roommate

This can be tricky. Believe it or not, your "best friend forever" may not make the best roommate. Many a friendship has been spared due to separate living quarters. Two loud and in-your-face people would most likely not earn back their security deposits if left alone as roommates. My college roommate was a girl I had known from my town, but she went to a different high school and we were not extremely close. We were great roommates, though. She was really sweet and mellow; I was more, well, not mellow. But we got along great, and we're friends for life. For many, opposites attract; although, in some cases, they don't. If you are a slob, don't hook up with a neat freak. If you are a lover of coed sleepovers, watch out for the more conservative types. Studiers should avoid partiers, etc. Most of these frightening combinations will be eliminated by a roommates' questionnaire, which many colleges send out with the hopes that five to ten random personality questions will produce matches from heaven. Kind of like eHarmony.

If your roommate preference is still blank, pick a decent place to live and have fun with it. Keep an open mind and you may be surprised about the new friendships you will make. Of course, you run the risk of getting paired with the person who showers maybe monthly, or the person who borrows (i.e., loses) everything with your initials on the tag; but if things get really violent, you can switch at the end of the semester. Most likely, you will meet at least one person in your suite or hall who will seem like your long-lost fraternal twin. Take him with you as you move on past that first year, and you'll have a great college experience.

Finances

Okay, this will be brief, as detailed money management tips are provided in Part Three of this book. But before you leave home, get your finances in order. Make sure you know who is going to pay your tuition, housing, food, utility, and insurance bills. Then make sure that person knows who and when to pay. Take whatever money you have saved out of the bank, and prepare to establish a new account. With the money you will be earning or receiving each month, plan a budget so you will survive. There is nothing more frustrating than financial stress coupled with being on your own for the first time.

Transportation

Getting from Point A to Point B will probably not be as hard as you may think. Keep in mind—most college students do not have their own cars! For the majority, check into getting a bike, or depending on your love of danger—a moped or motorcycle. You will be able to park closer to campus than any old driver of a boring car. If this is not possible, explore the facets of your local transit system. Bus fare is not that expensive, and buses run around the clock and to multiple locations. If you are too good to ride the bus, invest in a nice pair of running shoes and a back brace. (Bus fare's cheaper.)

Health Preparation

I must say that in four years of college attendance, I never heard a fellow student say, "Oh, I think I'll go get a physical today." Granted, things come up, and many flu-ridden students will moan their way to the campus clinic. In fact, one time I got a really painful plantar wart in my big toe (thanks to community showers), and I remember crying and limping back to my dorm after receiving an enormous shot ineptly given by some sadistic pre-med student—ow. Anyway, the time to take care of routine health care is before you leave. Get that last physical from your pediatrician, get your wisdom teeth pulled while Mom's still around to feed you Slurpees, visit that dermatologist one last time to rid yourself of those crippling traces of adolescent acne. Get it all done in your hometown, covered by Dad's insurance!

Time to Pack

Some people love packing and making lists. I am just going to assume you are one of those type-A personalities, you responsible person, you. But for all you left-brainers out there, hand this list to Mom, and have her stuff your new monogrammed bags. Just don't wait until the last minute!

- Pants/shorts/skirts/shirts/jeans (a must)

- Lots of socks and underwear (the more you bring, the less you do laundry)

- Pajamas, bathing suits, belts and hats—for 8 a.m. classes

- Jackets, sweaters, and snow clothes—if you're Harvard bound

- At least one formal outfit, or more depending on your social preferences (Most likely, your school will have formals, but no need to buy anything new since no one's seen your prom dress!)

- Shoes (for all kinds of weather)

- Accessories and jewelry (but leave Grandma's antique opal collection at home)

- Toiletries (the more you mooch from home, the less you'll have to buy)

- Bedding (sheets, pillow and case, comforter, favorite teddy bear)

- Towels and washcloths (some for bathing, one for swimming)

- School supplies: backpack, paper, notebooks, pens, desk-top supplies

- Computer/laptop, printer, ink and paper, if you're lucky; otherwise, check out the campus computer labs or your roommate's packing list

- Electronics: TV, iPod, phone, camera, alarm clock, lamp (but don't bring anything worth more than $200)

- Athletic supplies and clothes

- Reminders of home, pictures, decorations (don't go over-board; neither you nor your roommate needs to see your third-grade soccer trophy every day)

- Important documents: birth certificate, Social Security

card, visa/passport, medical record, insurance cards
(you will need these!)

- Waterproof, fireproof lock box or safe (for the above items)

- Address book

- Dishes, household items and furniture (depending on where you live)

Tips for Those on Their Own for the First Time

- **Don't bring too much**—you won't need it all, and you won't have the room to store it. But go ahead and check out storage options to pack away nonessentials at your new home. You can buy cheap shelves and storage bins at Wal-Mart or Target. Or consider raising your bed by placing the legs on cinderblocks for more storage space underneath.

- **Discuss with roommates who will bring what.** Believe it or not, you really won't need two refrigerators, toasters, and DVD players (unless you're an electrical engineering student).

- **Don't split large purchases with your roommates.** Spending $50 is much more alluring than spending $300 when going in on an air-hockey table, but you don't want to be a victim of the fist fight that breaks out over the thing when move-out time comes.

- **Don't get a pet!** Most colleges don't allow any pets on campus for good reason: you won't have time or money to take care of it, and you don't want to be tied down to your apartment to take care of Fluffy when everyone else takes a last-minute road trip. Even fish require weekly tank cleanings and daily feedings. Wait until you're married and baby-hungry to get a furry friend.

• Become friends with your resident advisor or whoever else has the power to forgive curfew violations and other "little rules."

chapter 2

The Four-Year Plan:
How to Plan Your Class Schedule So
You Can Actually Graduate by Twenty-One

Test your ability to graduate in four years:

1. In four years, I could:
    a. Read this book
    b. Write this book
    c. Have graduated from Stanford with high honors and begun my master's at MIT

2. Thought about a major?
    a. Yeah, my major thing is a spa pedicure!
    b. Easy, cheetah, I've got time . . .
    c. Chemical engineering with a minor in nuclear physics

3. How do you feel about seeing a counselor?
    a. Whoa, like, *I'm* not mental, but my best friend's cousin sees one and he says she's got total social anxiety disorder . . .
    b. What's in it for me?
    c. I will be confirming my expected course load for this semester with him at 4 p.m. next Thursday

---

If you scored:

Mostly a's: It will take you four years to read this book.
Mostly b's: You may have two senior years.
Mostly c's: You probably have a 30-year plan.

In a perfect world, the young, beautiful and fabulous would remain a carefree eighteen forever, kind of like a CW drama. But in the Real World, most young, beautiful, and fabulous people like yourself would like to get in and get out of college before wrinkle cream becomes necessary. However, graduating in an optimal four-year window is harder than it seems.

Very few students are on top of things enough to know exactly what their major is and how to graduate with a degree in it before they attend freshman orientation. In fact, most students at freshman orientation will end up changing their majors five times throughout their stint in college. Five times!

Some of you may wonder, "If college is just a four-year party at Dad's expense, why do I want it to end so soon?" Well, besides the obvious fact that the financier of college may not want you to prolong your festivities, there are other reasons. Most colleges encourage timely graduation so that other students can attend without overloading the school's acceptance limits. So as much as they may love you, they still want to replace you in four years. Some schools will even start charging you graduate student rates (which are higher) to get your slothful self out of there. Also, you may not care how long the chaperone-free fun lasts when you are a freshman, but by the time you are a senior, you will probably regret the time you wasted that is now preventing you from continuing on with the rest of your life. So when planning your class schedule, keep the number four in mind.

While the freedom you will discover in college is liberating, the reality of self-discipline will give you a good kick in the pants. No one will hold your hand and walk you through college, and if you don't earn sufficient credits to graduate, you won't be called a "failure," but a "professional student." And sure, you can take as much time as you can afford to graduate, but come on, what student wants to end up older than all the professors? Before you can create a plan that will allow you to graduate in four years, there are some essential things you need to know about how college is different from high school.

Report Cards

High School. You were sent home with a report card (that you hid).

College. Look it up—If you (or anyone else for that matter) want to know your grades, you'll have to check online or request a transcript.

Class Requirements

High School. There are certain courses you are required to take and generally you have very little choice—besides what level or type of math, English, or science you are ready for.

College. You will be expected to meet a certain amount of credit or unit hours before graduation to fulfill the requirements of both your college and your major. You will have many more options as to what classes to take.

Lunchtime

High School. Generally, high school is very structured; there is a certain place you are supposed to be at all times. You are even assigned when you can eat. You probably have to have a note to excuse absences and tardies, and there are punishments if you violate rules.

College. Free time! In college, no one tells you—or really cares—where you are or where you are supposed to be. This is good and bad. You set your own schedule, but it's also very hard to be your own boss. Ther is no one to blame but yourself if you miss class and fail finals.

Homeroom Teacher

High School. You probably had some sort of home base in high school where you heard announcements about what was going on.

College. You're on your own! There is no loud speaker in your dorm that will tell you your daily schedule and what time the assembly is. You will control your own level of awareness.

Lockers

High School. You used a locker to store your books and gym clothes, so you didn't have to carry everything all the way down the hall of your high school!

College. Now's the time to meet a good chiropractor, because if you schedule continuous classes, you will thoroughly enjoy your backpack workout!

Yes, the freedom of college life basically rocks, but you'll be so over it by twenty-eight. So now is the time to decide a few things—like what you want to study. You may be wondering, "What is this thing they call a major?" A college is a large institution of learning you will be attending, but it is actually made of several smaller colleges—or departments— that house the deans, professors, and classrooms of the major you will eventually pick. Unlike high school, in college you must pick a particular focus that you want to study. While you will take other general education classes, the majority of your time will be spent studying the field in which you are interested in pursuing a career.

The two main reasons people do not graduate in four years are because they don't pick a major until junior year (or change their major several times) and they take unnecessary classes "for fun." While cake decorating seems like a great way to consume free dessert and meet a member of the opposite sex who is bound to cook for you, it really is a waste of time unless it falls under your major's requirements. So how do you pick a major? Get out a sheet of paper.

1 **Assess your fate-granted situation.** Is Dad just dying to hand over the family business to you? Would you be willing to run it? College is still a great option—your degree can either be a back-up plan if things fall through or something that will just make you that much better of an employee or employer. Are you from a country club pedigree, and you just know that the trust fund grants you $20 million when you turn twenty-one? Still, get a major in something that interests you, so when you are living your life as a philanthropist, they can introduce you as the guest speaker who "graduated from Princeton with a degree in social work." If you are getting married fresh out of high school and know your spouse will support you until the world stops turning, don't be stupid—get a backup degree in home economics, if nothing else. You never know what might happen!

2 **Create an "interest list."** Granted, some people have known since birth that they want to be an astronaut or a veterinarian, but others may have a variety of interests they have considered pursuing. Make a list of all of your hobbies—the things you enjoy doing. If your hobbies don't extend beyond watching TV, consider the shows you watch. If you love *Law & Order,* write down law or police work as an interest. If you love the HGTV network, list interior decorating or architecture. Think of hobbies that you are passionate about though, not just things you find mildly intriguing. You will always do better studying something that really interests you.

3 **Reflect on your talent areas.** Was there a time in high school when you helped someone with homework and actually got through to the person when no one else could?

(I see bright red apples in your future.) Do nursing homes' residents' faces just light up when you walk into their room? (Do I hear social work? Medicine?) Are you awesome at basketball but not tall enough for the NBA? (Hey, coach!) Did you give the best speech in your high school's election history during student government campaigns? (There is a science behind politics.) Are you good at listening to people's problems? (Pull up a couch.) A great shopper? (Fashion merchandising actually pays!) Add these to your list!

4 **Take a career test.** Many high school and college counselors have access to tests designed to assess your areas of strength and weakness. These tests will evaluate your personality and specifically tell you several careers you may want to consider.

5 **Go to work!** If you still do not know if a career's right for you, go to an occupational site for a day and see what it's really like. Many nursing students didn't truly fall in (or out) of love until they changed that first set of hospital bed sheets. Ask several companies to let you observe their office or workplace for a day, or get an internship or part-time job in a field that interests you. Experience is the best teacher.

6 **The final test:** Once you have picked a major, find out a job description of the related career by interviewing an employee in that field. Discuss all of the aspects of the job. Find out the daily routine, the salary model, the travel requirements, the hours in a typical workweek, the job's benefits and downsides, what qualities it takes to succeed in that field, how much of a demand there is for people in that profession, and how hard it is to get hired and promoted in that field. Listen carefully to the answers to these questions, and consider how your personality and priorities match that field. If you feel confident (and hopefully excited) about what you have learned, proceed with your major!

Once you have chosen a school and a major, make sure they are compatible—don't go to a school without an accounting program if you want to be a CPA. Then, you need to plan out your course load for the next four years. A school counselor is the perfect person to help you do this, but if you are a do-it-your-selfer, here is what you need to know.

First, you will need to get three things: information from your college or university that tells you all the courses required to graduate, information from your department (your major) that tells you their required courses, and a course catalogue that lists all of the classes offered. Remember that the required hours you complete for your major also count toward those required by your college or university. When you make your schedule, also remember these semester-saving tips:

- You may qualify to test out of certain classes, based on your high school courses or achievement test scores. For example, if you scored highly on the math section of the ACT, or you got a 3 or above on an AP English exam, you may be able to bypass freshman math or English. Check with your college on what they require to override basic courses.

- Always take general education classes (those the university will require of you to graduate) first. This will prevent you from wasting time in classes for a major that you may later change. Plus, it will get classes out of the way early that you may not be interested in (biology, technical writing, calculus . . .).

- Beware of frequent transferring of schools. Sometimes the school you transfer to will not deem your prior school's courses as equal to theirs, and you will have to repeat the course.

- Don't get in over your head freshman year. My mom picked my freshman class schedule, which I learned wasn't a good idea when I found myself surrounded by juniors and seniors as the only freshman in three—yes, three—upper-level honors courses my first year. I'm glad she had such confidence in my ability to do well, but I was also glad that she took credit for the three C's I earned my freshman year. Only enroll in classes whose number begins with "1" your first semester. Those 202's, 318's, and 411's are exactly that—intended for second, third, and fourth-year students.

- Take as many courses as you can handle each semester. If you will be working or playing sports, however, you may not be able to handle a full course load. Here is a simple formula that guides you as to how many credits you should take each semester, if you want to graduate in four years: divide the number of credits required for graduation by the number of semesters in four years of college (eight), and that will equal the number of credits you need each semester. The college I went to required 128 total hours, so I tried to take at least 16 credits each fall and winter semester. You can always play catch-up by taking spring or summer term courses. Because I attended three summer terms (also a good idea if you want to get done early), I graduated in three years. That's another benefit of college over high school—you set your own pace.

- If you do want to put yourself through further academic stress, torture, and paper-writing misery by graduating with honors, decide your freshman year and find out all of the requirements of your school's honors program. You will be required to maintain a high GPA, take certain classes, and do other reading or volunteer work assignments. If you wait until your senior year to decide to do an honors program, it will probably be too late. Also, if you have a scholarship, make sure you are keeping up with its commitments.

- You may have the option of completing an internship (a short time spent working as an apprentice, possibly for pay, for a field you may eventually want to be hired in) or a semester abroad (in which you would complete special classes geared toward your major in a foreign country). If you want to have those experiences, decide early so you can plan it into your schedule and start saving money! While these are both great, rewarding opportunities, they can postpone your graduation date.

- Decide if you want a minor. A minor is another concentrated area of focus that you can study, but it requires fewer completed hours than your major. You do not have to have one at most schools. The benefit of a minor is that it shows graduate schools and companies looking to hire you that you are competent in more than one area. It is a good idea to minor in a foreign language, as we are living in an increasingly international society. If you do change majors halfway through your junior year, you may have achieved enough credits in your previous major to make it your minor.

- Pick classes based on the professor, not on the time! You will always enjoy class more, and thus do better in it, if you have a good professor. Ask upperclassmen which professors are known for daily pop quizzes on reading assignments—eek, and which are lazy about passing around the roll—yay!

- Try not to schedule back-to-back classes. You may be surprised to find how hard it is to get from building four to building twenty-eight in ten minutes. Do you really want to be the kid who comes into class sweating and wheezing everyday? Also, if you space your classes at least an hour apart, that gives you the perfect amount of time to catch up on homework, studying, or hallway naps.

- Are you a morning person? If not, don't enroll in 8:00 a.m. classes. Base your class schedule on your personality. If you are afraid to walk home alone at night, don't pick classes after 5:30 p.m. If you like to make nightly social rounds, stick to afternoon classes.

- Enroll early! You will be assigned a time when you can enroll for your classes by phone or online. If this time is at midnight, don't wait until lunchtime the next day. The best classes always fill up early, and you don't want to be stuck with that pop quiz-crazed professor. If you are not able to get all or even any of the classes you want, see if your college allows you to add classes. If so, follow the requirements so you can take the place of students who drop the class, or no-shows. When adding classes, it is best to be polite to the professor, rather than demanding that he or she add you. Remember the importance of that first impression.

- If you find yourself in a class that is just way too difficult, or just really not what you were expecting, you can withdraw if you don't wait too long! Check your university's requirements and deadlines for dropping classes as soon as you know you've got to get out, so you can avoid late fees.

- Apply for graduation on time! It sure wouldn't be pleasant to have completed all of your required courses and attend your graduation only to find your name is not in the program. So, check your school's requirements for graduation.

Okay, now we're ready to begin planning your schedule. Take out your lists of all the courses you are required to take and a pencil with a good eraser. To fulfill some requirements, you will have several options of courses you could take. Tentatively circle the ones that are most appealing to you.

Then, copy the following Course Planning Guide (p. 26) four times (one for each year), and begin to fill in the blanks. Start your freshman year with classes that you think will be the easiest, and remember, only take general eds, or required classes that could apply to a variety of majors. As you fill in the blanks, be sure to check the times of each class, so you don't overlap. As nice as it would be to take etymology, chemistry, and geometry all at once, it just doesn't work that way. Also, check the location of each class, and be realistic about how much passing time you will need.

Then, after picking the feasible times for each course, fill in your schedule using the chart on page 27. Post the chart where you can see it, until you memorize your schedule each semester. Once you have finished your freshman year, you can pencil in your intentions for the next three years. Of course, you should be flexible as this will change several times, but it is always best to start out prepared for what lies ahead. Good luck! We'll see you in four!

Course Planning Guide

Course Name
Professor
Location
Credit Hours

Course Name
Professor
Location
Credit Hours

Course Name
Professor
Location
Credit Hours

Course Name
Professor
Location
Credit Hours

Course Name
Professor
Location
Credit Hours

Course Name
Professor
Location
Credit Hours

Course Name
Professor
Location
Credit Hours

Time	Mon	Tues	Wed	Thurs	Fri	Sat
			Course/Location			
7:00 a.m.						
8:00 a.m.						
9:00 a.m.						
10:00 a.m.						
11:00 a.m.						
12:00 p.m.						
1:00 p.m.						
2:00 p.m.						
3:00 p.m.						
4:00 p.m.						
5:00 p.m.						
6:00 p.m.						
7:00 p.m.						

chapter 3

Schmoozing Your Way to an "A":
How to Convince Your Professor You're
an "A" Student—Even If You're Not

How "schmoozy" are you?

1. "Kissing up" is:
    a. What you do when you kiss someone taller than you are
    b. For people with no backbone
    c. The only way I get what I want

2. Someone with a "brown nose"—
    a. Should wash their face?
    b. Is so freakin' annoying
    c. Wow, this is such an amazing quiz! You're incredible!

3. Schmoozing is—
    a. Squeezing toothpaste from the middle
    b. For businesspeople
    c. Sweet talking, and man, am I good at it!

If you scored:

Mostly a's: You will marry a politician.
Mostly b's: You beat up politicians.
Mostly c's: You are a politician.

Okay, you may have answered all b's, and you may roll your eyes at anyone who even attempts to suck up to the professor, but I guarantee it doesn't hurt to learn a few tricks from someone who has gotten out of three speeding tickets and has talked her way onto the set of various TV shows.

Schmoozing is an art, and you'll quickly learn its benefits in college when it comes to your grades and the professor.

The Sacred Art of Schmoozery

Now, what do you think of when you hear the words "British literature?" Yes, the phrase even bores English majors. But that was the required predicament I found myself in junior year. I kid you not—Ben Stein's protégé was the professor, and it was held in a basement classroom with no windows and fluorescent lighting. Couldn't be worse.

I was having a particularly "off" semester (I had just gotten engaged), and I really didn't give a flip about reading *The Faerie Queen*. So, I decided to rely on my people skills, rather than academic achievement, to pass the course. I went to every single class (but did no homework), volunteered comments (that really made very little sense), but just smiled and nodded at every thing the professor said the entire semester. I was shocked mid-semester when the group I was paired up with made a slight reference to the fact that I was the teacher's pet—they didn't know I still hadn't bought the textbook. So I decided to see how far I could get with these little practices. Each class period, I noticed that I was the only student who made frequent eye contact with the professor. Though I miserably failed the few tests that were graded objectively, I left with a B+.

Still not an A, you may say. If you are a nail-biting perfectionist, there are a few other schmoozing tips that will fare you well with most college professors. I am giving you my no-money-back guarantee that these tricks will raise your GPA.

Know the Difference Between Teachers and Professors

Teachers care about how much you learn from them, and how well they teach. They like to feel as if they are making a difference in the lives of their students. Complement them, or even better—write a note, and let them know how much you appreciate their concern over your welfare as their student. Then, welcome to college. Professors like to do just that: "profess" their greatness to you. Unlike teachers, they generally don't spend all of their free time making up cutesy lesson plans and visual aids. They are busy researching and writing, getting published and giving lectures. They are omniscient, wise PhD's and they are not afraid to let you know it. So, let them know how great you can pretend to think they are. Read one of your professor's publications that isn't on the required semester list, then discuss its ingenuity with its masterful creator after class one day. He'll remember it—and you.

"Getting to Know You . . ."

No teacher or professor is capable of rewarding their star pupils with higher grades, unless they know their names. Your instructors will announce their office hours at the beginning of the term, or in their printed syllabus. Know them; use them! Make at least one visit to the office at the beginning, middle, and end of the course. The first time, introduce yourself and shoot the breeze. The other times, review your answers on an exam, or ask for special help with course material. Professors will usually be a little more lenient with students who go out of their way to ask for "extra help" or who "don't get it." Use these phrases for your creative benefit. Be sure to always introduce yourself again, as professors have many more names to remember than you do. Then, make a point to sit in a very visible location in the classroom—preferably near the front. Every instructor usually has a "buddy" he pays more attention to throughout the class, and that person always has a front-row seat.

Smile and Nod—A Lot

Are you nicer to crabs or puppies? No one wants to coddle a crab, but people go ga-ga over puppies—why? Because puppies have a happy-go-lucky, irresistible presence. People like to receive a warm reception—especially when they are "performing," which is essentially what teachers do. If you ever look around a classroom when a teacher is lecturing, you'll notice most people are drooling, texting, or watching the hands on the clock. Be the person who always maintains eye contact with the professor. Yes, the constant smiling and nodding may make you somewhat annoying to your peers, but your professor will just eat it up and reward you handsomely for being such a great lapdog.

Be Opinionated

Have you ever dated someone who just blindly agrees with everything you say? Not very interesting. Professors are always drawn to people with strong opinions, as long as their opinions are based on logical facts. Believe it or not, most professors are confident enough in their position that they can handle a good debate or disagreement. When a question is thrown out into the classroom and you have a comment that is somewhat intelligent, voice it. But always be able to support it with evidence or reasoning. Most professors will respect an outspoken, intelligent student, even if they disagree with you.

Do It Their Way

Always follow a professor's directions exactly. Don't use a rigid teacher's writing class to be "creative" with orange gel ink on the essay test. Each assignment you receive will have guidelines—follow them step by step. If your professor is slightly vague in her instructions, refer to the syllabus or specifically ask what she's looking for (another good excuse to take advantage of office hours). Teachers do appreciate creativity, but not when it means they have to read cutesy verbiage in weird fonts on purple paper.

Adopt a Class Role

Okay, so you don't *have* to be the brown-nosing teacher's pet. Be the class clown or the class question asker. As a former teacher myself, I know that every class has a personality with its own unique individual personalities. A teacher depends on those personalities to carry the class. Certain people adopt roles, and if they are not too aggravating, the teacher (and students) will miss them when they're absent. I went to a very strict, conservative college that had a rule that males couldn't grow their hair longer than their collar line. In a political science class I took, there was a guy who had shoulder-length hair. At the beginning of the semester, the teacher commented on this; but after two class sessions, he no longer cared, because the long-haired guy was so funny. He became the reason people came to class, and at the end of the semester, people (including the professor) were actually sad when the guy cut his hair.

Go to Class, on Time, Every Day

Enough said. But if you have to be late, do it inconspicuously. Slide in the back and sit down in the nearest seat that doesn't require you to have to make someone else stand up to let you through. If you know you are going to be absent, tell the professor beforehand and try to get his understanding as well as any make-up work you may need to complete. It is also a good idea to have one buddy in every class to call if you are absent, so you don't miss a pop quiz announcement.

Never Cause Unnecessary Distractions

Most professors would agree that it's a good idea to turn off cell phones, pagers, curling irons, and iPods while in class. Try to refrain from neurotic twitches, tongue clicks, and any other common fourth-grade bodily noises while in a quiet room. Leave your ice crunching, gum chewing, and wrapper crumbling until you are outside. And heaven forbid, never read a newspaper openly during a lecture—I once witnessed a guy get thrown out of class permanently for such behavior. Don't be the back-row whisperers, or the note passers, or the pencil, paper, and homework borrowers. While it is a good idea to adopt a class identity, don't be the annoying one who everyone wants to be absent.

Let Them Know You Care About Your Grade

The old adage applies—"The squeaky wheel gets the grease." If you feel like whining because you think a grade was unfair, make an appointment to talk with the professor. During said appointment, do NOT whine and say, "My grade's not fair!" Instead, create some logical reasons why you feel you were wrongly graded and present them in a very mature, respectful manner. If you think there were too many trick questions, don't accuse the professor of trying to trick you. Instead, say something like, "I feel this question was particularly ambiguous or open-ended. Could you please clarify what you meant?" Also, remember that the professor is not the only person who may be judging your work. Often, instructors have teaching assistants who may be grading your papers. In that case, showing your grade to a new party (the professor) may fare you well. Several times I protested a grade and my squeakiness was awarded with a better grade on that paper and the next one.

Don't Ask Dumb Questions

You may have heard the phrase, "There are no stupid questions." I beg to differ. Many a time I have heard students ask really idiotic questions that annoy the tar out of the professor. Don't ask questions that are dumb, lazy, or which have answers that are provided in the syllabus. Samples include:

- Will this be on the test?
- Do we have to buy the book? (especially if the professor wrote the book)
- Do we have to do the homework?
- Do we have to type it?
- When will our tests be graded?
- Have you graded our tests yet?
- Will our tests be ready by our next class?

Never Cheat or Plagiarize

There is no quicker way to get on the hit list of a professor than to prove he can't trust you. In fact, many universities will expel you with even one instance of cheating. It's just not worth it. Don't let the pressure of good grades overwhelm you to the point that you're willing to give up your integrity. Grades don't matter that much. Besides, in most cases, the amount of time people spend organizing their cheating plots would be more than enough time to study effectively.

Don't Overdo It

If you try too hard, not only will you annoy your peers, but the professor will run from you, as well. Don't go overboard with the teacher's pet role. I'm sure you've met people like this. Don't volunteer to cut the professor's lawn, or wash his windows, or grade everyone's test. And while we're at it, don't be one of those really annoying curve setters—you know, the person who gets a 98 on everything so all of us 81ers still wind up with a C.

Schmoozing is an art that can be perfected with a little practice. It is best done in person, smiling, and in an admiring, yet non-disturbing way. And it really will pay off in other areas of your life. For instance, admiring your mechanic, video store clerk, and dentist can get you free car washes, video rentals, and toothpaste! All it takes is a little schmoozery . . .

chapter 4

Writing Tips Even "-ology" Majors
Need to Know

How gooder our you at writting?

1. What comment do teachers usually scribble on
    your papers?
    a. Masterpiece!
    b. Good effort...
    c. How many times did you fail kindergarten?

2. What's wrong with this sentence?
    "fred lovs pickles"
    a. Capitalize the f, "lovs" is misspelled,
        and put a period at the end
    b. Ew! Pickles are gross!
    c. Looks good to me!

3. The word "ain't"
    a. Should not be used in formal papers
    b. Is often used in Mississippi
    c. Is purty, ain't it?

If you scored:	
Mostly a's:	Welcome back, Shakespeare.
Mostly b's:	Don't skip Writing 101.
Mostly c's:	How many times did you fail kindergarten?

While Shakespeare is dead, writing lives on. It is used by all literate people, in all fields. So, if you absolutely hate to write and picked zoology as your major in hope of avoiding a research paper, too bad! While I'd pick writing over dissecting pigs any day, many people gag at the thought of outlines, topic sentences, and revision. And even great writers experience the occasional writer's block or are stumped by the guidelines of MLA documentation. The following tips will hopefully initiate you into the basics of college writing. After you have copied each of them down ten times onto your steno pad, advance to section two, where we will together endure a little writer's workshop. I promise you that if you pay attention, your writing scores will improve, your professors will gape at your literary skills, and the world will stand in awe of the genius that is you. (Was that convincing? Persuasive enough? Read on!)

Basic Writing Guidelines Every College Student Should Know

Always Type!

Gone are the chicken-scratched essays and journal entries your high school English teachers undoubtedly loved. An understood rule in college is that all of your assignments should be typed. And even if typing is not required by a certain professor, do it anyway! If you do not have your own little PC, check with your roommates or other friends to see if they wouldn't mind sharing. If they do let you borrow their computers or printers, always save the file to your own disk—don't clutter their hard drives. And if you'd like to keep your computer-lending friend as a friend, always offer to buy or split the cost for that person's paper and ink, because that stuff is expensive! If you don't know anyone who owns a computer (not likely), or who is willing to share and isn't using it himself (more likely), check into using your school's or local library's computer labs. You may have to pay a small fee and work on their time schedule, but your improved grades will make it worthwhile.

Follow All the Directions of the Assignment

Your instructors should provide you with information detailing the guidelines of each assignment. Don't lose that information! What works for one professor may not work for another.

Be Professional

When "I have a paper" time approaches, you will most likely see one of the two following acronyms in your professor's instructions: MLA or APA. These refer to the two most commonly used stylistic guides for research papers. Each style follows a particular format for in-text citations, endnotes/footnotes, and reference pages. Generally, the MLA (Modern Language Association) format is used for the liberal arts and humanities, while the APA (American Psychological Association) is recommended for the social sciences. There are books and websites that provide all the information you need to successfully follow each style, so find them, know them, use them.

In general, assume that all your papers should be double-spaced, on 8 ½" x 11" white, standard paper with 1" margins on all four sides, in black ink, and in the English language. Indent each paragraph (by pressing "tab"), and justify your margins to the left. For a simple paper, don't include a cover page; just write your name, your professor's name, the class and section, and the date on the first four lines on the left side of the first page. Then, center your title on the next space, and begin your paper. Use a "header" to place your last name and the page number in the upper right corner, one ½" down from the top, of each consecutive page. Always include a reference page, if outside sources were used.

Find Out the Grader's Style

Yes, believe it or not, your highly paid (ha!) professor may not be the one reading and grading all of your papers. You do need to find out the personality type of whoever is holding that red pen. Some graders will only care whether or not you completed the assignment. Others will massacre your paper and leave all of your grammar and spelling mistakes bleeding. Don't get discouraged—it's easier to mark the errors than the praises of a paper, which you'll find is true when you are assigned to do peer revision. Just make sure that for papers you submit, you know what to focus on to get a good grade.

Finish Your Paper at Least Twenty-Four Hours Before It Is Due

Make sure you give your work time to sit before you hand it in. When you separate yourself from the work, your subconscious clears itself and allows you a fresh, objective approach when you complete your final read-through. Also, this gives you the safety of having your paper completed, printed and ready to turn in early enough to avoid last minute Murphy's Law situations. Nearly everyone has encountered a crashing computer or inkless printer five minutes before a deadline. Avoid this with the twenty-four-hour rule.

Find a Proofreading Buddy

There is bound to be someone in your hall who is an English major. Offer free pizza to him if he will look over your papers. You can even form a peer editing group, or go to your school's writing lab for a tutoring session. Even if you feel you are a qualified writer, always take the time to get another person's perspective.

Save, Save, Save!

Save all of your papers onto your hard drive as well as a disk. And while you are working, press the save key often.

Learn from Your Mistakes

When you get a paper back that, well, wasn't quite so perfect, review the red marks. Internalize what the grader critiqued; and though you may disagree with the feedback, try to learn from it. Otherwise, you will never improve. If a professor notices that you attempt to amend your areas of writing weakness throughout the semester, he may decide your final grade based on your final writing attempt, rather than that bloody thing you got back the first week of class.

And Now We Enter the Writer's Workshop

Okay kids, we are going to cover the four essential aspects of writing a paper: the writing process, the parts of a paper, technique, and style. I guarantee this will be the easiest writing class you'll take all semester.

Writing Process

Not all papers will require you to accomplish every task, but here are the general steps to take when you receive a writing assignment.

1 **Pick a topic.** Unless you are assigned one, select a topic that you find interesting, because then you will do better work. Make sure it is not too broad or narrow. And be sure to stick to your topic throughout your paper.

2 **Gather your research.** Collect sources from the library or Internet, and write down interesting facts that apply to your paper. Don't forget to document the sources for your reference page!

3 **Create an outline.** Based on your research, divide your paper into subtopics and make a detailed outline, assigning your researched facts to specific sections of the paper.

4 **Write a draft.** Following the organization of your outline, write a rough draft of your paper with an introduction and thesis, body paragraphs, conclusion, and reference page.

5 **Proofread.** Check for any errors in spelling, grammar, usage, punctuation, documentation of sources, and other mechanics. Make sure you followed the directions of the assignment.

6 **Revise and submit!** Focusing on organization and clarity, read through your paper and revise. Also, let a classmate or the writing lab offer revision tips. Then let it sit for a day, correct any final problems, and turn it in!

Parts of a Paper

Title

The title is what draws your reader in to your paper, and hopefully awakens a grader who has already read through forty-plus similar papers before yours. Your title should make the topic of your paper known in an interesting way. For instance, if I were writing a paper on U2, I could title my paper, "U2: A Band That You Can't Leave Behind."

It is sometimes best to wait until you are done with the paper to pick a title, using a catchphrase or central idea of the paper as a title. Your title could also be a question your paper answers or a variation of your thesis sentence. Many titles are two phrases separated by a colon, like *Real World 101: A Survival Guide to Life After High School*. For an essay or paper, do not underline, italicize, or put quotation marks around your title. Simply center it at the top of the first page.

Introduction

If your title woke up your professor, your introductory paragraph should convince him to ingest even more caffeine. Your introduction should be fresh, informative, inviting, even funny. Start by stating an unknown fact about your topic, or include a brief joke, a relevant quotation, or an anecdote. End your introduction with your thesis statement.

Thesis Statement (or Topic Sentence)

The thesis statement is the paper's central idea that you will be proving or expounding upon throughout the body of your paper. A good thesis statement is straightforward, narrow, and should show the organization of your paper by mentioning the subtopics you will be discussing. Try not to make your thesis too factual or too opinionated, but give it some oomph!

Body

The body of your paper should consist of several paragraphs that discuss the subtopics of the thesis. Include a topic sentence and a clincher for each separate topic you mention. You want your paper to flow from idea to idea, so be sure to use transition words like "additionally," "for instance," "in contrast," and "finally." Don't include information that isn't relevant to your thesis, but at the same time, try to eliminate wordiness. I promise your professor will be more impressed with concise, coherent thoughts than dozens of multisyllabic words that neither you nor he knows the meaning of.

Whenever you include information that you obtained from an outside source, whether it is a direct quote, a paraphrase, or a restatement of someone else's ideas, you must cite your source. The MLA way to do this is to simply place the author's last name, a space, and the page number in parenthesis at the end of the statement but before the end punctuation mark like this: (McAlpin 41). If you mentioned the author's name in the sentence, simply put the page number in parenthesis (41).

Conclusion

Ah, finally! Your conclusion need not be long—just a short paragraph that ties all of your points back to the thesis. You may want to throw in one final thought or quote about your topic. Just don't leave the reader hanging or wondering where the rest of your paper is.

Reference Page

If you consult outside sources in your paper, you must document them in a reference page. Before we go there, I want to quickly mention one thing. Surely you have heard of some dastardly daring person who has attempted to submit a paper he obtained over the Internet. Gasp! Seriously though, it happens all the time. But what also happens all the time is those people get caught, fail the class, and are sometimes expelled from school. So don't do that or any other form of the "p" word of writing—yes, plagiarism. Plagiarism is using someone else's ideas, whether directly or indirectly, without giving that person credit. It is a punishable crime, and professors do have ways of sniffing it out. So, always cite your sources! And this is how if you are using the MLA format.

Write "Works Cited" at the top of the page—minus the quotation marks. Double space this page, and alphabetize your sources. Align the first line of each entry to the left, but indent subsequent lines until you start a new entry. Generally, you will arrange the information in this order: put the author(s) name (last name first), then a period; the title of the article (if applicable) in quotation marks, period; the title of the publication underlined or italicized, period; the publisher's name, colon; city in which it was published, comma; then the year it was published, period. Here is an example works cited page with two sources, one a magazine article, and one from a book:

Works Cited

Backrow, Bob. *Get Me Outta Here*. Downtime Press: New York, 2006.

Frontrow, Farley. "Writing Papers is Wicked Fun." *Scholar Magazine*. Westwood Publishing: Chicago, 2009.

Technique

"Technique" is a broad term that we are going to use to cover a variety of topics that produce groans at their mere mention in English classrooms across the country: sentence structure, punctuation, capitalization, usage, and spelling. Now, now, stop your whining, and pull out your photographic memory.

Sentence Structure

All sentences have four requirements. They must do the following: (1) Be a complete thought; (2) have a subject and a verb; (3) end with a punctuation mark; and (4) begin with a capital letter.

When writing sentences, avoid fragments (incomplete thoughts, often missing a subject or a verb) and run-ons (sentences that do just that—go on and on and on). There is an exception to the fragment rule, but of course, you'll find there is an exception to every rule in the English language. But in contemporary writing, people often use short and even one-word sentences for dramatic effect. This is okay as long as it is done correctly, as in the following line: *"Tall. Dark. Handsome. She read each word as if her dream..."*

Punctuation

You've learned them all before, but here is a quick review of the most commonly used punctuation marks.

Period (.): ends sentences that are statements or commands; used for abbreviation (Mr., Dr., P.O.W.)

Question mark (?): ends sentences that ask a question

Exclamation mark (!): ends sentences or words that show a lot of emotion

Colon (:): connects related words or phrases; used before someone introduces further examples or information

Semi Colon (;): joins two related clauses or sentences; separates lists that contain long phrases

Quotation Marks (" "): indicate quoted material; used for titles of shorter works; emphasize specific words

Single Quotation Marks (' '): used for quoted or emphasized words within quotation marks

Ellipsis (. . .): shows that material has been removed

Parenthesis (( )): indicate material that is an after-thought or is non-essential; used for documentation of sources

Comma (,): used to separate phrases and clauses; separates items in a series; sets off quoted material from the rest of the sentence; used after words that address someone

Apostrophe (’): shows possession; indicates that something was deleted in contractions; used to make awkward words and numbers plural (8's)

Hyphen (-): used for compound words; used after some prefixes; used in words that start on one line and continue on the next

Dash (—): sets apart non-essential material; indicates hesitations in speech

Front slash (/): separates fractions & phrases like "and/or"

Capitalization

Always capitalize:

The first word of every sentence; **C**apitalize this letter.

Names of specific places, persons, or things; **M**cDonald's, **S**usan

Titles used as part of a name; **P**resident Roosevelt

Geographical names; **L**ondon, **G**reat Lakes

Familial titles that refer to a specific person; **U**ncle Joe, **G**rammy

Names of institutions; **L.S.U.**, **L**ee **L**ibrary

Specific courses (and all languages); **M**ath 101, **F**rench

Things found on a calendar (besides the seasons); **M**ay, **T**hanksgiving **D**ay

Brand names; **X**erox, **M**icrosoft

The term "usage" broadly refers to how a writer should use words. There are a few common problems writers have in their papers that can be avoided if you review these rules after every paper you write.

1 **Avoid misplaced modifiers.** Modifiers are words or phrases that are supposed to make writing more clear, but often do not when placed after the wrong word in a sentence. Always place a modifier directly next to the word it is describing, as in these examples:

Wrong Jane fed her turtle, the girl next door.
Right Jane, the girl next door, fed her turtle.

Wrong Washing cars, the parking lot was crowded.
Right The parking lot was crowded with people washing their cars.

2 **Don't shift tenses.** Remember the grade school phrases: "past tense," "present tense," and "future tense?" Yes, after all your years of schooling, it's still a good idea to pick one tense and stick with it for each paper you write. Writing in the present tense is usually the best way to go, as it makes your writing more engaging to the reader.

3 **Keep an active voice.** The "voice" of the paper can be active or passive; stick to active. In passive voice, items are acted upon rather than committing the action, which makes for stiff writing. Instead of this: *Our dinner was cooked for us, then set upon the table.* Try this: *Mom cooked our dinner, and set it on the table.*

4 **Keep your writing parallel.** Parallelism is using similar language for expressing ideas, so that your writing is more clear. Instead of saying this: *I love to run and cooking.* Try this: *I love running and cooking* or *I love to run and to cook.*

5 **Make sure your subject and verbs agree.** If your subject is singular, don't make your verb plural, and vice versa. Instead of this: *She run to school each day.* Try this: *She runs to school each day.*

Spelling

One word: Spellcheck!

Style

When you really want to impress your professor, your style will be the element that does it. Style in writing is basically adjusting your writing voice to the assignment's level of formality, while keeping in mind your audience. Some graders prefer informal, even humorous writing, while others are looking for more traditional, formal styles. In informal (or colloquial) writing, you can write as if you are speaking directly to the reader to revive your writing. In more formal papers, however, avoid personal pronouns (I, you, we, etc.) and slang words or expressions (kinda, like, got, etc.) that would indicate you are speaking directly to the reader. When you are assigned a paper, ask yourself, "What type of assignment is this?" Following are the five basic writing assignments you will receive in college and their respective levels of formality that the professor will expect.

Narrative Writing—real or imaginary story, journals, letters, poems. *Light-hearted, informal, as if you were speaking.*

Persuasive Paper—debate/trial speech, editorials, issue papers. *Convincing, factual, semi-formal, strong language.*

Descriptive Writing—descriptive paragraphs, character sketches, poems. *Literary, provides detail, uses figurative language.*

Reader Response—personal response, subjective essays, journal entries. *Personal approach, open for interpretation, uses figurative language.*

Expository Essay—research papers/essays, how-to papers, news articles. *Formal, informative, factual.*

Now that wasn't so bad, was it? Write a persuasive paper to your college and tell them you memorized this chapter—and maybe they'll let you out of freshman writing!

chapter 5

Hitting the Books
(in a Nonviolent Way)

How hard do you hit the books?

1. The last book I read was:
   a. *War and Peace* (for the third time)
   b. Do *Cliff's Notes* count?
   c. *Green Eggs and Ham*

2. My idea of studying for a biology test is:
   a. Flashcards, study groups, tutors
   b. A quick twenty-minute cram
   c. A $5 cheat sheet

3. This quiz was:
   a. A breeze
   b. Somewhat challenging
   c. What was the question?

If you scored:

Mostly a's: Skip the chapter.
Mostly b's: You should have studied for this quiz.
Mostly c's: You should have cheated on this!

After you unpack your luggage, go to orientation, and attend your first official college party, you may be dismayed to learn that there is more to college than fun. Yes, you will one day find that you will have to . . . study!?! A lot of people spend their whole freshman year figuring this out, then spend the next three or more years working to redeem their freshman year GPA. I must admit I was not a big studier in college, but I made up for it by being organized, cramming, and learning how to B.S. my way through an essay test. I didn't graduate with honors, but my GPA was above a 3.0. However, if you want to go to grad school, I recommend "studying" these study tips.

Get Organized!

Pick whatever organizational device you prefer (Blackberry, day planner, writing on your hand), and use it! Every professor should give you a syllabus at the beginning of the semester that will list when all of your homework, reading assignments, tests and papers are scheduled. Get ahead by entering all of this information for all of your classes for the entire semester in your calendar. Then you will be able to look ahead and know what weeks will be busier than others. I'm pretty convinced that professors all get together and pick two dates out of the semester, then schedule all major assignments and tests on that day. It's a conspiracy. I can just hear them laughing at their office parties: "You scheduled your final the same day as my fifteen-pager is due, right? Har, har, har, I can't wait to see the dark circles under their eyes!"

Enter all of the social events and extra-curricular activities you plan on attending on your calendar, as well. Every night before you go to bed, review your schedule for the next day, to make sure you haven't forgotten about any quizzes, meetings, or hot dates. This will engrain your schedule in your mind and help you be better prepared for the next day.

You will need certain supplies for college, but don't expect to receive a "school supply list" in the mail like you did in elementary school. You will probably do best by buying a large three-ring binder, filled with dividers labeled for each class and stocked with plenty of extra paper. Always take this to all of your classes, along with a pen and pencil (and maybe a few extras for any cute, needy classmates).

Set Goals For the Semester

To really be a great student (and person, for that matter), set goals for each semester. Your goals do not all need to be academic, though. You could set financial goals like "get a job"; or social goals like "make three new friends," or "join a club." To be successful, a goal should be the following:

- **Specific.** "To run better" is not as effective as "Run three miles a day."

- **Measurable.** How far will you run?

- **Challenging.** Do you already run three miles a day? Stretch yourself!

- **Realistic.** If you currently only run one mile a day, give yourself enough time to work up to three.

- **Written down!** So you remember to run!

Know your learning style

If you look around a typical classroom, you'll see people doodling, tapping their feet, staring off into space, taking notes, and probably sleeping. There is an educational reason to justify all of this—besides the sleeping. People have different learning styles. There are three different kinds of learners: visual, auditory, and hands-on. Each type has a style of learning that is most effective for him. By reviewing these types, you should be able to recognize what type, or even types, of learning styles you have and the most beneficial ways you can process information.

1. **Visual**—likes to "see" what he's learning through visual aids (diagrams, drawings, colors, artwork, flashcards, outlines)

2. **Auditory**—has to "hear" himself repeat information to process it (oral repetition, debates/discussion, listening to tapes)

3. **Hands-On**—has to "feel" the knowledge by hands-on interaction (lab experiments, skits, role plays, computer programs)

Note-taking skills

As you yawn through class every day, you will notice that everyone around you is taking notes because lecturing is the basic teaching style of every professor you will ever encounter. Exciting, huh? But, taking notes gives you answers to test questions, so pull out your pen and take notes on these strategies!

• **Neatness counts!** Save the M.D. calligraphy for when you're a real doctor. Be neat in your note taking, because I know (from the squinting I am now doing as I try to type this from my notes) that you will be less eager to read messy notes than neat ones. So, write on the front side of the paper only and leave plenty of space below each point you write down, so you can go back and add information later.

• **Only write down key words.** Your professors will talk much faster than the average writing speed. Unless you were a secretary in high school, don't attempt to write everything down. So, if you were going to take notes on this tip, you would not need to write down all of this babble, just the words: "Only write key words." At the same time, don't be too sparse—you want to remember what the professor was talking about.

- **Get to know at least one person in every class.** That way if you miss a class, you have someone who will let you copy his notes, and vice versa. (Or even better, get someone to fall in love with you in your stadium-style classes who will always let you copy their notes, and you can squeeze a nap in each day! Don't tell your mom I said that.)

The Library

Agh! At the very mention of the word, I have nightmarish flashbacks to freshman year, when my school required that first-year students take a "library test." There is no better way to stand out as an amateur in college than to walk around five floors of bookshelves wearing headphones while writing down random library trivia. But, you really should check out the library before you graduate from college. There are all kinds of resources there like periodicals, microfiches, reference books, atlases and almanacs that will help you with papers and projects. My personal recommendation is the "literary criticism" section, in which you can find articles annotating every major literary work—just call them the *Cliff's Notes* of college.

Reading Strategies

If you made it all the way through twelfth grade without learning to read, your secret will be discovered in college.

In college, the word "homework" really means "reading." Yup, that's all you will do in every class, besides math. But even there, you will probably have to skim a few articles on famous mathematicians and the history behind their proofs and theorems. Just keep in mind that when you are assigned to read a chapter, you do not have to read every single word. In fact, if you did, you would never find time to eat, sleep, or go to class, because I have been assigned as much as 150 pages to read per night per class. Rather, use these strategies to help minimize your reading time:

- **Survey the material.** When assigned to read a chapter, look through it first to see how long it is, how many sections there are, and what is really the meat of the assignment. Then you can focus your time on what you think will count for the most points on tomorrow's quiz.

- **Focus on the bold print.** Look at the chapter headings and sub-headings, and any bold words, pictures, graphics, or charts that are emphasized. Focus your energy on understanding the significance of them.

- **Speed-read.** Speed-reading is really just teaching your brain to notice any word with more than four letters. Quickly skim through the text, ignoring the little filler words. But, make sure you are mentally paying attention to the big words when you do this.

- **Underline/outline/take notes.** Reading material does you little good if you have nothing to show for it. Highlight key passages, make an outline, or write a brief overview of everything you read.

- **You be the professor.** As you read, ask yourself, "If I were the professor, what questions from this material would I put on the test?" You'll be surprised at how many of your questions actually show up on the test!

Study Skills

Although studying isn't the prime social event on anyone's calendar (I hope), a few skills can minimize your studying time while maximizing your studying success. You should pick study times, environments, and methods that work for you.

Times

Are you a morning person or a night person? Use that to your advantage. Try to schedule set times to study each week that work well for you. For memory retention, it is best to study a little bit each day rather than procrastinate until you are forced to pull an all-night cram session before a final. However, review all of the material right before you go to sleep, and again first thing in the morning before you take a test because while you sleep, your brain continues to process and internalize what you read.

Environments

No matter how focused you are, frat parties, cafeterias, and Disneyland are not good study environments. You need to find a place that works best for you. One day while walking home from a class at my university, I discovered . . . the law library. It was clean and newly decorated with fluffy furniture and dim lighting. There was a fraction of the students there than at the regular library, and it was more inviting than my own apartment. I marveled at my discovery and claimed it my studying turf. I even had my own little loveseat I sat in near the same window each time I went. I became a law library groupie, mentally mingling with the future litigators of America from my little den.

On my way home from classes, I would head straight to my corner, sit in my couch, open my books, and—fall asleep.

The problem was that it was too quiet, too clean, and too comfortable. I then discovered that I do much better studying at a place that I don't want to be! So, back to the hard chairs, dirty tables, and muffled whispers of the campus library.

Think of the factors that affect you negatively and positively when you study. Eating? Background noise? Cold or warm temperatures? Bright or dim lighting? Soft or hard chairs? In groups or alone? Put together a list and stick to it. And make sure you stash your cell phone so no text message interrupts you.

Methods

There are several different ways to study. When you have a lot of material to review, the first thing you should do is prioritize. Which test is most important? What do you know will be on the test? Which parts of the test will be worth the most?

Obviously, budget your time and spend the most time studying things of the most importance. Write down how much time you will spend on each area, and always study the hardest subjects first. If a study session is scheduled, definitely go, because it will be a harem's nest for free answers.

Remember your learning style when deciding which study method is best for you. Making flashcards and mnemonic devices is great for visual learners. Auditory learners benefit from reading material to themselves repetitively or putting the facts they must know to a song. Hands-on learners can do something active in a group setting or make a visual replica of what they are learning.

Test-Taking Skills

Test time is here! You have five minutes to prove how ready you are. Take this test to see if you've got a chance to pass those college exams.

1. When going to take a test, I think my attitude should be _____.
   a. Positive so I try my best to do well.
   b. Um, yuck! Who likes taking tests?

2. When I go to take a test, I should take _____.
   a. A pen or pencil and a Scan-tron or a test-taking booklet.
   b. A cheat sheet.

3. When I first see the test, I should _____.
   a. Skim through the whole thing to budget my time and know what to expect.
   b. Groan as I realize I brought the wrong cheat sheet.

4. When I see the word "directions," I should _____.
   a. Read and follow them—especially key words like "compare/contrast," "list examples," and "write a brief essay."
   b. Ignore them. I follow my own instructions!

5. If I don't know an answer, I should _____.
   a. Make an educated guess using process of elimination and explain my reasoning in hopes of getting some credit.
   b. Guess C?

6. When I get a test back, I should _____.
   a. Review what I missed, ask the professor to explain anything I don't understand, and keep it to study for future tests.
   b. Crumple it up and throw it away—who needs a reminder of failure?

If you scored:

Mostly a's: "A" is the letter you will be seeing in your future!

Mostly b's: Bad, bad boys and girls!

chapter 6

Justifying Socializing as Social Work:
Ways to Build a Good Resume

What kind of a job will your resume get you?

1. Your dream job is to be a _____.
    a. Stay-at-home dad
    b. Sales clerk
    c. C.E.O.

2. Your most significant volunteer work was _____.
    a. Getting take-out for my boyfriend after a long day's work
    b. Raking Grandma's leaves
    c. A two-month service expedition in Peru

3. You could obtain a decent letter of reference from _____.
    a. Pete's Pet-Sitting
    b. Pizza Hut
    c. The Police Department

If you scored:

Mostly a's: Packing specialist at FedEx
Mostly b's: Pilot-in-training at FedEx
Mostly c's: President of FedEx

There will come a time in your life when a resume will help you—whether it is for a college technical writing class or for an internship with the CIA. A resume is a brief listing of your accomplishments that should convince an employer that you are qualified for a particular position. While you should never lie on your resume for more reasons than one, it is possible to embellish your skills history to place yourself in a more positive light. For example, the term "babysitter" is not quite as impressive as a "childcare professional." If you were voted "Sorority Sweetheart," you may want to consider retitling yourself "Elected Representative of Prestigious Society." Try to see the potential of everything you have done as something that is really important, and your future employers will see it that way, too.

It is always good to have a resume on your hard drive, ready to update whenever you may need it. Resumes are actually quite simple to make, especially with the resume templates that most basic software programs provide. So before starting from scratch, consult your PC for help. But, if you haven't upgraded your computer since the Olsen twins split from Full House, here are the basic do's and don'ts to creating a decent resume.

Presentation

Do: Prepare your resume on a white, 8 ½" x 11" piece of typing paper (that means type it) in black ink with a standard 12-point font like Times New Roman. Separate the sections with bold print and simplistic lines, if necessary.

Don't: Be cutesy and include colors, graphics, slogans, or drawings. Pink, perfumed resumes featuring butterflies and balloons do not impress inhabitants of the real business world.

Professionalism

Do: Use formal language and keep your resume to the

point. List the job you are seeking and form an objective curtailed to that description.

Don't: Include overly personal information that shouldn't affect your ability to get the job like age, marital status, former salary, disabilities, connections you have at the company, race, height, weight, pets' names, and favorite colors. And don't attach a photo unless requested to do so.

Length

Do: Keep your resume minimal in length—one page should be sufficient for most jobs that do not require extensive technical or specialized skills. Only include information that is applicable to the position you are seeking.

Don't: Ramble on about unnecessary facts of your life. Only include information that would potentially help you get the job you are seeking. Never submit a resume longer than two pages.

Heading

Do: Top your resume with your name, address, phone and fax numbers, and an email address.

Don't: Include more than one address or two phone numbers. And don't include a link to your family blog.

Objective

Do: Place your mission statement or occupational objective at the top of your resume so that employers see you as a goal-oriented, productive person.

Don't: Ramble on for more than one sentence or use language that is too simple or too precocious. Be concise yet creative.

Format

Do: Pick a format for organizing the divisions of your resume by making it chronological, functional, or both. A chronological resume lists your professional and educational history in reverse chronological order, and includes the dates during which you worked at each job or attended each school. A functional resume focuses more on your skills and abilities and how they pertain to the job you are seeking than the dates you completed them. You can combine the two by listing your experiences in chronological order, while also detailing your skill level in each area.

Don't: Jump from one random experience to another. Try to keep your resume parallel and orderly.

Required Subheadings

Do: Include the subheadings "Experience" and "Education" in your resume. For experience, list your work history. Be specific by mentioning where you worked, the dates you worked there, the position(s) you held, and the duties you fulfilled. For education, list the high school and college you last attended and any degrees you obtained. Also, include any vocational or specialized skills training you have received. Only include your GPA and any special academic honors you achieved if they are flattering to you. Despite what you may think, employers aren't impressed with GPA's below 2.0.

Don't: List every job you have ever held (they probably won't care that you mowed lawns when you were eleven), and don't include the names of your grammar schools, or more than one high school and two colleges (unless you have earned graduate degrees).

Optional Subheadings

Do: Include other headings like "Hobbies and Interests," "Volunteer Work," and "Awards and Achievements" if you have significant things to list in these areas, especially if they relate to the job you are applying for. Appearing well-rounded doesn't hurt your image.

Don't: List more than three hobbies (you don't want to appear as if you have too much free time) and five service experiences or awards. Avoid listing anything that relates to shopping, talking on the phone, and hanging out with friends.

References

Do: List the names, titles (Dr., Professor, etc.), addresses, phone numbers, occupations, and relationship to you of two or three people who are familiar with your personality and work skills.

Don't: List anyone who does not like you, or anyone who you are not sure of what they would say about you. I once managed a swimming pool, and my least favorite employee (he truly earned this rank) listed me as a reference on his resume. Well, make sure you ask your boss if she will be a positive reference before you list her, because I'm sure that my opinion of the guy did not help him get the next job his prospective employer called me about!

Cover Letter

Do: Introduce your resume by attaching a professional cover letter that acts as a sales pitch for you. Include the position you are applying for, and list a couple of reasons why you are qualified and why you would like to work for the company.

Don't: Summarize your entire resume in the cover letter. And don't forget to be professional!

Okay, now you get to be the employer. Following are the cover letters and resumes of two applicants for the same job—a referee for a community sports league. Which one would you hire?

Employee #1: Luke Laidback

Dear Coaches and People in Charge,

I totally think I am the right person for your job. I have had all this experience with sports and stuff. Like I play sports, and I watch them all the time, cause I have ESPN, and somet8imes I even watch classic sports, where you can check out these gnarly games from, like 20 years ago. I don't have a car right now, but I can skate over in good weather.

I haven't really worked before—well, but I had this job once mowing my neighbor's lawn, but I only did it for a few weeks because she told me we had "different artistic styles" or whatever, and I was just like "Okay, whatever lady." But I could be a really good worker cause I think it's important to be on time and stuff. And I like to watchkids play sports, even if they're not that good, cause most of them really aren't, but anyway, give me a call, and I'll come over and we can talk figures and stuff.

Later—Luke
You can catch me at 555-9876 (or just look for me at the arcade)

Schools I went to:
Harbor High School (but I didn't finish there, I got my GED the next year.)
Palmdale Community College (I went to a few classes, and got an A in soccer—yeah!)

Work Experience:
Mowing lawns (for a neighbor for $40 the first time, but after that she would only pay me $20).
And that's about it

Things I like to do:
Skate (Or die man), Eat (Fritos, Subway, and corndogs), Watch Sports (I'm so the person for this job!), Play soccer (I learned how at college), Sleep (hey, who doesn't), I like the ladies, if you know what I mean. Pick me! Pick me!

(Hmm . . . Quite unimpressive, don't you think? Very unprofessional, informal, filled with typos and slang. Not much experience, and does not seem to be reliable. He may be a fun person to hang around with, but not someone I would hire.)

Employee #2: Scott Stable

Scott Stable
112 Dependable Drive
Hiring, NH 09800
(968) 555-1432

Jim Jobgiver, Director
City of Hiring Youth Sports
334 Main Street
Hiring, NH 09876

Dear Mr. Jobgiver:

In response to your ad seeking youth sports referees, I hope you will consider me for the job. A former Hiring youth athlete myself, I would love to work for your organization and gain this valuable employment experience.

I have been an avid sports fan my entire life, and have played baseball, basketball, and soccer for my high school the past three years. I am familiar with the rules of sports, and would love to spend this summer vacation as a Hiring referee. I appreciate your time and consideration.

Sincerely,

Scott Stable

Objective: To gain a valuable employment experience in a field
          I love.

Experience

Footlocker Sales Clerk   2008-2009
 •   Sold athletic supplies to customers
 •   Maintained the cash register and store

Lloyd's Lawncare Landscaping Engineer   2006-2007
 •   Maintained neighborhood yards
 •   Dealt with appointment setting and
     customer service

Education

Hiring High School   2007-2009
 •   Junior Honor Student, 3.7 GPA
 •   Member of baseball, basketball,
     and soccer teams

Awards

Eagle Scout   2006
Hiring High School Freshman of the Year   2006

Reference: John Murrow, Manager at Footlocker
(968) 555-3456

(Hmm . . . Now there's a good candidate. For a junior in high school, he sure has presented a professional resume. He includes interests and job experience that prove he would be right for the job. He seems to be respectable, smart and athletic. I can always check with his former employer to see what kind of a worker he is, but I think he may be a referee this summer!)

A good resume is the key to getting a good job. So remember, be professional and creative, and you will prove to the employer that you are the right person for the job!

Good luck—whether you're applying at Taco Bell or Texas Instruments!

part

2

Surviving Your First

Home Away from Home

chapter 7

Playing House

What message is on your doormat?

1. What supplies would you need if you moved?
   a. A garbage sack
   b. A few boxes and some duct tape
   c. Boxes, packing tape, bubble wrap, change of address forms, some rope, a truck, a few friends . . .

2. C. O. stands for _____.
   a. The stuff you sniff at the dentist's office
   b. Colorado
   c. Carbon Monoxide, a deadly poison—yikes!

3. Your home best resembles which holiday feeling?
   a. Halloween fright night
   b. Independence Day—anything goes!
   c. Christmas pines and presents

If you scored:

Mostly a's: Go Away!
Mostly b's: Um, what doormat?
Mostly c's: Welcome

When you were a kid, did you play house? School? Or doctor? (Naughty, naughty!) Whether you remember it or not, you owned a plastic kitchen set at one time or another. And in this little playroom scene, you were either Mommy, staying home to take care of Cabbage Patch Kids and cook mud pies all day; or Daddy, cast off to the backyard by the neighbor girls and forced to sit on the patio holding a pretend briefcase until Mommy and her "babies" agreed it was suppertime.

Times have changed. Roles have merged as many men are cooking and cleaning, and even more women are carrying the briefcases. But whatever uniform you put on each morning, it is important to be self-sufficient in the home, because you never know which role the Real World will hand you. Both men and women need to be familiar with terms like U-Haul, ADT, and Martha Stewart to create an optimal home environment. To really make your house a home, here are three classic touches to haul through the front door, whether it be your first move or your fifth move; your first apartment or your third house; and whether you are a boy or a girl.

A Mover's Touch

Your first moving day may seem simple, as you have nothing more to lug out to college or your first apartment than a few bags of clothes and your Ikea bedding. But as you get older and collect more stuff, moves will become more elaborate, time consuming, and expensive. So, try not to move too much (unless you get one of those really great jobs that provides you with a moving allowance). Following are seven important issues to consider when planning a move:

Professional Movers vs. Do-It-Yourself?

When it comes to moving, you can hire a moving company to come in, pack up your house, load up the truck, drive it to your new place, unload, and put all your things in the right place. Sounds great, huh? Why would anyone not move that way? Because the price tag is anywhere upwards of several thousand dollars. So unless you have a couple grand burning a hole in your pocket, you will probably have to join the rest of us in a nice, cheap, do-it-yourself move.

There are two ways you can move yourself. You can rent a truck (call Budget, U-Haul, or any of the other moving company trucks you see driving around in your area on Saturday mornings), but you will need to reserve it well ahead of time. You may also want to rent a dolly and furniture protection cloths. If you are moving locally, you will probably be able to rent the truck for less than $80 a day, plus mileage—but don't let that "low price" fool you. Mileage can add up fast and is usually anywhere from 50 cents to a dollar per mile. Plus, you'll have to fill the truck with gas before you return it, and boy, do those things guzzle! If you do a long distance or one-way move, the truck will cost a lot more, so make sure you fit everything into one trip, and that the rental company knows you will be dropping the truck off at another location.

But renting a truck and all that equipment is still more convenient than your last option, which is the hard-core do-it-yourself method. You know your "friend with the truck?" Everyone has one. Call him up and offer a box of Krispy Kremes as a fair trade—after all, what are friends for! Doing it this way may take several trips back and forth, but is the cheapest option by far.

Change of Address

At least a week before you move, stop by the post office and pick up a change of address form. Fill it out with your new address—if you know it. If not, consider renting a P.O. box at the post office in your new town to collect your mail until you get settled. You can also change your address online at websites like *www.moving.com* and *www.usps.gov.*

Packing up your belongings should not be left until the night before the truck arrives. Plan well ahead of time how many boxes and how much bubble wrap you will need, and how your things will be packed. You can buy custom-made moving boxes with built-in compartments for all your drinking glasses and shoes at truck rental stores, but they are super expensive. A cheaper option is to drive behind local grocery and super stores and raid the recycled box dumpsters—I've done this many times. As long as the boxes were not tomato cartons in their previous life, they should be in pretty good shape. Best of all, they're free!

Bubble wrap is available at stores like Target and Wal-Mart, where you will also want to pick up a few rolls of strong packing tape, some permanent markers, and rope. It is best to pack up your house one room at a time, one section at a time. Label every box with two items of identification—in large letters, write the name of the room it should go in at your new residence. Then below that, in smaller letters, write a small, detailed list of the general contents of the box (for example: Bedroom—linens, cosmetics, books, Pez collection). I have a friend who is so organized that she set up a "moving database" on her computer and printed a list of every single item that went into every single numbered box. While she may have had moving dreams (or nightmares) for weeks before the big day, I guarantee she knew that she could find her Go-Go boots in Box 44c, if the occasion arose. And by the way, don't pack up essential items (toiletries, underwear, packing tape) until the day before your move!

Valuables

Wrap any item that you even think is valuable or breakable in clothes, linens, tissue paper, or bubble wrap, and label the box "Fragile." Keep all valuable items like expensive jewelry, heirlooms, financial statements, and your wallet with you throughout the move. You can even purchase mover's insurance—check with moving companies on how to do this. Just don't risk losing your valuables.

Storage

When you plan your move to your new place, consider whether you are going to have enough storage space. If not, call ahead of time to rent a storage unit. Pick a unit that is neither too big nor too small for your stuff; but if you find yourself deciding between two sizes, it is always better to go bigger than smaller—you never know what else you may need to store later on. Make sure you choose a storage company that has security features, and further protect your valuable items and electronics in the storage unit by placing them in the rear of the unit behind your house plants and linens. Storage units usually rent on a month-to-month basis, and the monthly fee can be anywhere from $30–$200, depending on the size of the unit you select.

Setting Up Utilities

Before you move, be sure to cancel your utilities (electricity, gas, water, cable, telephone) so you don't wind up paying your replacement's bills. Likewise, call a few days ahead to set up the utilities at your new place, so they are working when you get there. There is nothing worse than unpacking by flashlight and using your new neighbor's phone for three days. To set up utilities, check the Yellow Pages to see which companies are commonly used in that area, and call far in advance to schedule a new service. Don't call anyone with a company name like "Mom and Pop's Electricity," because your lights might run on Mom and Pop's sleeping schedule. You will have to pay deposits from about $50–$100 for some utilities, but many companies refund this amount after a year, if you have proven responsible about paying your bills.

For Sale

To move, you are sadly—or joyously—going to have to give up your old place. If you are renting and you are at the end of your contract, this may be as simple as wishing your landlord and roommates farewell. If you are in the middle of a contract, you will need to check into subletting (passing your contract on to someone else), or you'll have to find some other way to weasel your way out of it.

If you own your home or condo, you will need to consider hiring a real estate agent or posting a "For Sale, By Owner" sign in your window. Hiring an agent will make your move much easier, but agents also take out a fat cut of the sale price as commission. However, this may be the better option if you are looking to move quickly and to avoid any legal entanglements.

When either you or your agent has arranged to show your property, you have a much better chance of getting your asking price if you add some fresh paint, fix anything that is broken, remove any clutter (pack it up if you have to), and pop some homemade bread in the oven. You can improve your "curb appeal" by landscaping your yard, washing your outside windows and doors, and painting your exterior, if necessary. The better the condition of your house when you present it, the sooner you can post your "Sold" sign!

A Father's Touch

When your family heard the usual (yet somehow still frightening) bumps in the night, who picked up the baseball bat or butcher's knife and trudged down the stairs ready to defend his family from the threats of the evil ice maker? Yup, Dad—or any other brave soul who surely never believed in monsters under the bed as a child. Someone has to protect the house, and guess what? When you move out on your own, that person is you. There are better ways to keep your home protected than stealing a neighbor's security system stickers and placing them on your windows. Get in the habit of following these safety precautions:

- Lock all your doors and windows, whether you are home or not.

- Use the peephole to see who is knocking on your door before you open it!

- Request identification from service providers before letting them in.

- Replace the locks whenever you move to a new place.

- Use a fireproof box or safety deposit box to store your valuables and important documents like birth certificates, car titles, etc.

- Only put your first initial in the phone book, and don't use your answering machine to advertise when you are not home.

- Don't let all those people who drive slowly by your property know when you buy your big screen by placing the empty box on the curb.

- Consider getting a security alarm, motion detector lights, a guard dog, or one of those pretend barking dogs that detect motion.

- If you have a gun or other dangerous weapon, always keep it locked and away from children or other people who don't need to know about it. But make sure you know to use it safely, if necessary.

Away from Home

When you do venture out, always:

- Keep a light, TV, or radio on a timer to ward off intruders.

- Have a neighbor pick up the mail and newspapers, so the mail carrier (they can go postal) doesn't know you're away. You don't want a stack of *New York Times* piled at your doorstep, advertising that you are away in New York.

- Keep a car (yours or a friend's) parked in your driveway.

- Before you go away, make sure your hot water heater, air conditioning, and heater are left at levels that will conserve energy but also keep your pipes from freezing.

Fire Safety

The old "Stop, Drop, and Roll" technique you learned in grade school still works, but here are some other grown-up ways to protect your home from a fire:

- The National Fire Protection Association recommends installing a smoke detector on every floor and outside each bedroom. Make sure the batteries aren't dead by testing each alarm once a month.

- Have a Fire Escape Plan for your home. If it is more than one story, keep a roll-up ladder in each bedroom and know the quickest way out.

- Keep a multi-use fire extinguisher in your kitchen, and know how to use it.

- Use UL- and FM-approved appliances, and regularly

check your cords and plugs for fraying.

- Keep water away from electric currents.

- Don't overload your circuits with appliances.

- Store flammables in metal containers away from any heating equipment.

- If you do have a fire that gets out of control, call 911 immediately, get everybody out of the house, and remember if you're on fire: "Stop, Drop, and Roll!"

Carbon Monoxide Poisoning

Carbon monoxide is a tasteless, odorless, colorless gas that injures and kills more people each year than any other chemical substance. Fuel-burning devices can produce toxic levels of carbon monoxide and should be maintained safely. Check that the following carbon monoxide producers are not being used carelessly at your home:

- Fuel furnaces (check for cracks in the furnace)

- Cars parked in a closed garage and left running (never do this!)

- Stoves and fireplaces (keep them clog-free and turned off when not in use)

- BBQ grills (never operate them inside)

- Gas dryers, water heaters, and engines

- Cigarette smoke

To prevent CO poisoning, install a carbon monoxide detector on each floor of your house. These can be found near the smoke detectors at hardware stores, and you can even purchase a combination smoke/CO detector. Also, try to keep your house well ventilated when using fuel-burning appliances. If you do suspect CO poisoning, turn off the suspected culprit, get to fresh air immediately, and go to an emergency room if you feel you were heavily exposed.

A Mother's Touch

What really makes a house a home are the lessons learned from Martha and Mom. Every home has a mood—a feeling you get the moment you walk inside. What do you want the mood of your home to be like? Open and airy, or cluttered and festive? Old-fashioned and craftsy, or modern and cosmopolitan? Warm and inviting, or cool and comfortable? Do you prefer antique wood furniture or bean bag chairs and blow up couches; plush loveseats, or leather recliners? Do you like the atmosphere of the beach? The jungle? The desert? Or the mountains? Is your home messy and lived-in, or sparkling clean? The appearance of your home says a lot to others about you. How does your home affect the senses (besides taste—hopefully) of your visitors, and how can you improve the ambience?

Sight

When an interior decorator first walks into your home, she will notice the color scheme and décor. While many nineteen-year-olds couldn't tell you the color of the rug they are standing on if their eyes were closed, as soon as you do care what your place looks like, there is more you can do to create an aesthetically pleasing view than throw a few posters on the wall. Painting your walls is actually a lot easier than you may think, and it makes a world of difference in a room.

The colors you choose to decorate set a mood. Blacks, greys, and whites are more modern but can appear drab if not used correctly. Warm colors like reds, browns, and yellows are happy and bright but can give you a headache, if overdone. Cool colors like blues and greens are generally the most popular accent colors with decorators because of their widespread relaxing appeal. Spice up any room by adding a few candles, picture frames, lamps, plants, and books. You can also get an eclectic mix of decorations at flea markets and garage sales, but pass on the clutter.

Touch

The textures in your home are most evident in your furniture. If you are a warm, affectionate person, you may want to portray this through plush sofas, chairs, and beds, decorated with lots of pillows and throw blankets. You may want to carpet hard floors or use area rugs. If you wish to bring the outdoors indoors, use leather, suede, and other natural, simple fibers. Flooring also affects the feel of your home, as wood is warmer to the touch than tile but also higher maintenance.

Smells

Nothing distinguishes your home more than its smell—especially if it's bad! Taking out your trash regularly and cleaning out the refrigerator will keep things fresh. Open your windows when the weather is nice to let in the air, and keep a Bath and Body Works Wallflower or scented candle on standby in case company comes around.

Sounds

Is the TV always blaring in your house? Can your neighbors three blocks down feel the vibrations pumping from your amplifiers at any given moment? These may be a couple reasons why your house repels visitors or why it is always picked as the party location. The kinds of entertainment and tones of voice used in your home will affect the crowds who visit. If you want to have a quiet get-together, a little soft background music is always great; but a big party is dull without something upbeat pounding from the surround sound. Music is the ultimate mood-setter and a great way to express your style. So turn it up (or down) for your next event.

Now it's time to really play house. Whether you pull out that apron or go hide in your backyard—it's all up to you!

chapter 8

Windex, Pledge, and Other Strange Bottles You'll Find Under the Sink

How would Mr. Clean react to your place?

1. I Pledge _____.
   a. Allegiance to the flag
   b. To always love you
   c. My wood furniture

2. Windex is _____.
   a. The temperature when the wind blows
   b. A deck of cards at the Wynn
   c. An ammonia-based cleaning product

3. A feather duster is _____.
   a. One of those old-fashioned pen things?
   b. The perfect accessory to my French maid costume!
   c. The only way to really dust ceiling fans

If you scored:

Mostly a's: He'd be all over your floor.
Mostly b's: And your walls.
Mostly c's: He'd be all over you.

Okay, so maybe you don't own a vaccuum. Or a mop. Or a sponge. In this day and age where time is money, you may find it more advantageous to hire someone to clean your house than to do it yourself. But you always appreciate your things much more when you take care of them yourself (your mom told me to say that).

Learning how to clean your house is actually a really important life skill, especially when you need to impress your dorm's resident advisor, a potential roommate, and eventually that significant other who may become your roommate. And cleaning your house can be quite rejuvenating. Nothing beats the feeling you get after you've taken out the proverbial trash. Okay, enough psycho-babble. Let's get down and dirty.

Basic Cleaning Strategies

1. Establish a cleaning schedule—a set time each week that you will devote to cleaning. During that time, eliminate distractions by silencing your cell and shutting down Facebook.

2. While cleaning, listen to upbeat music or a book on tape to keep you going.

3. Start at the top and work down. Cleaning from the top of a room down will use gravity to your benefit, though you may wind up with quite a pile on the floor!

4. Keep all of your cleaning supplies in a bucket or basket and carry them from room to room to prevent unnecessary backtracking.

5. Clean as you go! Get in the habit of cleaning up after yourself daily. Never leave a room without putting something away, and take belongings upstairs rather than stacking them at the bottom. Instead of putting your glass in the sink, put it in the dishwasher or wash it right

away. You'll have to do it sooner or later, so you might as well take the time now so you don't freak out when company comes!

Get Organized and De-Clutter!

Ever heard the phrase, "Every thing has a place and every place has a thing?" Your granny-bug or some other meticulously clean person in your life probably said it to you the last time she tripped over the shoes you left in the middle of the living room. I can just see her now, shaking her head and pointing her finger, "Shame, shame, shame!" But, household cleanliness is a mindset—some people have it and some just don't. The benefits to keeping a clean, organized house are that you will always know where to find things, your life won't be as stressful, and you won't die of humiliation when people unexpectedly drop by. Plus, you probably won't lose things as much, and you won't forget important meetings and get-togethers because you can't find the invite.

Do you have random mail and handouts lying around everywhere? I once visited some friends who kept their mail right next to the toilet—their credit card statements made for an interesting substitution for *The Bathroom Book*. Keep up with your paperwork. Spend two minutes every night throwing out junk mail and sorting the other stuff as urgent and non-urgent into a mail divider or desk trays.

Then move on to the clutter goldmine—the closets. Dub a rainy day "The first day of my organized life" and go behind every closed door in your house. Put every single thing that you have not used or worn in the past six months into a box or garbage sack (you may need more than one). Don't get carried away by sentimentality—you may have fond memories of your very first Mickey Mouse snow globe, but it really is nothing more than a dust collector. When you're done collecting, put the container of useless items away where you won't see it for awhile and duct tape the box closed. Don't label it with anything more than the words "Discard in _____" and fill in the blank with the date six months from now. When that time arrives, donate the entire bag to Goodwill or another organization that benefits the less fortunate, without opening it, because then you'll just reminisce about the potential functionality of your footie pajamas. This may be difficult, but I guarantee you that you will feel much better afterwards in your new, uncluttered house.

Maximizing your storage space is another great way to make the closet-opening experience less depressing or dangerous. Start with a mild investment in storage compartments, shelves, hanging dividers, and other organizers you can find in home stores or at The Container Store. You can build shelves in your closets and cupboards. Consider adding a hanging bar to your closet underneath your shirts to double your hanging possibilities. Desk drawer organizers also work nicely as cosmetic, toiletry, and jewelry compartments.

You can keep your closets more aesthetically pleasing by always neatly folding and hanging clothing and linens. Hang your clothes by type (shirts, pants, sweaters, etc.) and color. This will also free up a little "getting-ready" time in the morning because you will know exactly where everything is. If you live in a place where the seasons demand different wardrobes, pack away your off-season clothes in storage containers to free up some hanger space.

Fold and put away towel and sheet sets together in your linen closet so when company comes, you can set out neat sets that match and charge them your bed-and-breakfast rate!

Cleaning Products

I have many times received blank stares upon asking male friends where they keep the cleaning spray after clumsily dropping an egg on the floor or spilling a drink. Many newly independent young adults do not purchase cleaning products, as if the chemicals are deadly upon purchase. To really deep clean a house, however, you need to stock that cupboard under the sink with the following products or create your own, with the nineteenth-century tried and true recipe that follows. Most of the products are available at your local grocery store, cost less than four bucks, and turn brown things white again! (Caution: Never mix bleach and ammonia-based cleaners, and keep all cleaning chemicals far away from your face!)

- **Glass Cleaner** (Windex)—Cleans glass (duh). *One part ammonia diluted with three parts water.*

- **All-Purpose Cleaner** (Lysol, 409)—Cleans counters, sinks, toilet exterior, tile. *Pour ½ cup apple vinegar in a bucket with warm water.*

- **Furniture Spray** (Pledge, Endust)—Apply before dusting for a thorough clean and shine. *Use the vinegar solution above (do not apply directly to wood, lightly dampen a cloth with the solution).*

- **Air/Carpet Freshener** (Glade, Arm and Hammer, Febreeze)—Absorbs odors. *Dampen a cotton ball with vanilla extract or perfume and set in a room; a box of opened baking soda set out or sprinkled in your carpet will also absorb odors.*

- **Mildew/Mold Remover (OxiClean, Lime Away)**—Eats the grime that nothing else will. *Soak mildew in vinegar.*

- **Toilet Bowl Cleaner (Comet, Lysol)**—Removes ring around the rim and other unmentionables. *Dilute one part bleach with three parts water.*

- **Cleaning Rags/Feather Duster**—Applies cleaner to surfaces. *Use old t-shirts, socks, and rags.*

- **Brooms/Mops/Toilet Brush**—Eliminates dirt. *Just get the real thing.*

Top to Bottom

And now, it's time to start—top to bottom. The first time you do a full-scale clean out, it will take awhile. But after practice, it will get easier and faster.

Windows

It is best to wash your windows when it's cloudy outside, so you can see the streaks, and avoid letting the sun dry the glass cleaner. From a distance of about 6 inches, lightly spray the window with a glass cleaner and wipe top to bottom with a dry cloth. Change your cloth often to minimize streaking. Or, you could use a water spray bottle and squeegee to wipe off the dirt; just make sure to wipe your squeegee dry after every swipe. Wipe your window sills with a moistened rag, and use the brush attachment on your vacuum to dust your blinds. Every six months or so, take your blinds and screens outside and scrub them with soapy water.

Walls and Doors

If you have flat wall paint on your walls, unfortunately the only way you will be able to clean them is to paint over the dirt. But, for most other walls, doors, and baseboards, dampen a cloth in warm water and wipe. This will give your home a very quick, noticeable pick-me-up as the gray smudges disappear. You can use a mild cleaning solution on some walls and doors, but test it first in a not-so-noticeable spot. Never apply anything with bleach to colored paint or wallpaper.

Dusting

Again, start at the top and work down. You can dust your ceiling fans and light fixtures with wet wipes or damp dusting cloths. Eliminate corner cobwebs with a vacuum extension or broom. For most wood furniture, you can lightly spray Pledge, Endust, or a similar product onto a soft cloth, and rub it into the furniture in small circles. Don't use any chemical product on antique or delicate woods without testing it first in a discreet place.

Bathroom

Always keep an all-purpose cleaner or Lysol wipes and toilet bowl brush in your bathrooms, in case unexpected company stops by. At least once a week, you should deep clean your bathroom, unless you're conducting a science experiment on the different types of mold and mildew. Before you start cleaning, sprinkle Comet or apply a toilet bowl cleaning solution to the inside of the toilet bowl, and let it soak while you clean the rest of the bathroom. Then, clean the mirrors and any chrome fixtures with a glass cleaner and soft cloth. Next, spray the counters, sink and exterior of the toilet with an all-purpose or tile cleaner, and wipe with a cloth. The easiest way to clean your tub or shower is while you are bathing, because the steam will help loosen the dirt and mildew and you don't have to worry about getting your clothes wet. You will need a strong tile and tub cleaner or mildew remover and scrub brush for the tub. Using a squeegee will eliminate water spots from your shower walls and doors. After your shower is spic and span, brush the inner toilet bowl, and then finish the bathroom by mopping or scrubbing the floor with a cleansing solution. Done!

Kitchen

The first step to cleaning the kitchen is to clear all of the dishes, food, and clutter off the counters and table. Load your dish washer, or wash your dishes by hand and put them away. If you want to clean your oven (you brave soul), follow the directions on the back of a spray oven cleaner. If you are lucky enough to have a self-cleaning oven, it should be as simple as spraying the oven cleaner, turning the knob to the clean setting, and leaving while the fumes do the work. Otherwise, you'll be scrubbing for awhile. The next step is to spray everything with an all-purpose cleaner and wipe your counters, table, and chairs. Then dry all surfaces to avoid water marks. Scour your sink with hot water and a cleanser made for tile or stainless steel. Then, wipe down your refrigerator and appliances with a cloth dampened with water and an all-purpose cleaner. Finish with the floors.

Floors

Regularly sweep the dirt off your hard floors and deposit it into the garbage with a dustpan. Then, deep clean according to the type of floor you have. You should be able to mop tile, linoleum, and plastic laminate floors like Pergo and vinyl with a cleansing agent diluted in a bucket of warm water. After applying the soap, rinse with water and dry with a towel to avoid streaking and slipping. For wood floors, always check with the manufacturer for proper cleaning instructions, as moisture can warp some types of floors. A vinegar solution or special wood cleaner is usually the best solution for wood floors.

Carpet

Vacuum your carpet often to maintain its long-term appeal. But nothing makes your house look and feel as clean as a deep carpet cleaning. You can hire a professional, but it will cost enough that you may want to keep a carpet spot cleaner like Folex on hand for the in between stains that will occur between major cleanings, which should be done about once a year. When cleaning your carpets, whether by yourself (rent a machine at your local grocer and go to town) or a professional (the easier choice), keep in mind that there are several carpet cleaning methods: spot cleaning, dry cleaning, steam cleaning, chemical cleaning, shampooing, and foam cleaning. Check with a carpet company to find out which method is recommended for the type of carpet you have. After cleaning, you should not walk on the carpet for several hours to allow it to dry completely. If you plan to hire someone, remember you get what you pay for. All those ads you see that advertise two rooms for $15 do the kind of job that lasts about fifteen hours!

Odor Removal

Once I moved into a house in which the previous owners had allowed their three cats to use the place as their personal litter box. Believe me, as someone who is allergic to cats, I know about odor removal! In extreme cases such as these, you will probably want to have the air ducts cleaned or even get the place fumigated, so that heavy odors and dander don't constantly circulate throughout your house.

To remove the smell of smoke, place a bowl of vinegar in each room of your house, and it should suck up the odor. Charcoal briquettes placed on newspaper can absorb some pet odors. If you want to zap those mysterious kitchen smells—like those in your refrigerator—dip a cloth in lemon juice and wipe the surfaces. Baking soda is also an effective odor remover. Always keep a few spray deodorizers or scented candles on standby, for when that special someone comes over. But the overall best way to prevent odors is to keep your house clean—and now you know how, so no excuses!

chapter 9

Get Your Security Deposit Back:
How to Handle Basic Home Repairs

How handy are you?

1. Landlords are _____.
    a. Mystical creatures from The World of Warcraft
    b. Fat, bald men who read dirty magazines
    c. Responsible for maintaining my apartment

2. Spackle is _____.
    a. A box of fishing supplies
    b. A WWF move
    c. Painter's putty

3. A plunger is _____.
    a. A skydiver
    b. A large person who jumps off a diving board
    c. Something that unclogs toilets

If you scored:

Mostly a's: Keep the handyman on speed dial.
Mostly b's: Don't. Touch. Anything.
Mostly c's: Whatcha doing Saturday morning?

Every time I went to a friend's house to play as a child, my mother would call after me, "Leave things better than you found them." Plagued by my mother's admonitions, I was always the dorky kid left straightening the money in the Monopoly game as all the other kids had moved on to Candyland. While this phrase tarnished my childhood reputation, it has paid off when dealing with landlords and security deposits.

When you sign a rental agreement for a condo, apartment, house, trailer, houseboat, refrigerator box, or whatever else you decide to live in, you will most likely be asked to provide a security deposit. A security deposit is an amount of money (usually half of or equal to the amount of one month's rent) that will be refunded to you upon termination of your contract, if you did not damage the residence in any way. Many landlords will deduct a standard minimal amount out of every security deposit for carpet and house cleaning or fresh paint. But, if you leave your residence better than you found it, you should get all of your money back. So after packing, loading, and hauling all of your junk out of there, make sure you do the following:

- Deep clean the place (and now you know how).

- Leave all furniture, appliances, light fixtures, and other home accessories where they were when you moved in.

- Buy some painter's spackle, and use it to fill the empty nail holes (cheap alternatives to spackle: putty, tooth-paste, and gum).

- Make sure all the light fixtures have working bulbs.

- But if your apartment is in really bad shape, you may want to consider . . .

Painting

Painting isn't brain surgery—it's actually an easy do-it-yourself way to freshen up your place whether you are moving out or not. Just check with your landlord first to make sure it is okay. To paint, you'll need:

- Paint! (make sure you are using the right sheen and color)

- Drop cloths (old bed sheets or newspaper also work well)

- Roller brush, paint pan, and paint mixing stick

- Painter's tape or a brush designed for edges

- Turpentine (in case you spill paint on the carpet)

- A long rolling brush and ladder (if you are painting tall walls or ceilings)

For a basic paint job, follow these steps:

1. Prep the room by moving furniture and pictures away from the walls. Put drop cloths on the floor by the wall's edges and over any furniture that may get in the way. If you do not have a paint edger, stick painter's tape along the edge of the surfaces bordering where you intend to paint. For walls with a base paint that is latex, satin, or eggshell, wash the walls first with a damp cloth.

2. Open your paint can and stir with a mixing stick. Pour a small amount into your painting pan until it is about 1-1 ½" deep.

3. Roll the paint roller in the well of the paint pan until it is evenly saturated, but try to roll off any excess paint along the top of the pan.

4. If you are painting your ceiling, do that first. Next, paint each of your walls, rolling the brush up and down in even strokes. Try to complete each section within a short time period so it dries evenly. For the edges, use a paint edger or a small brush. After it dries, apply a second coat and you're done!

Broken Glass

If your roommates' Final Four living room tournaments got a little too rough, or if the local Romeo literally climbed through your window, your landlord may find it beneficial for you to remove the broken glass to prepare it to be replaced. Be very careful when doing this to avoid getting cut. In fact, if the window has/had very large panes of glass, it is best left to a professional. But, if you are going to do it yourself, make sure you wear a thick pair of gloves that cover your wrists, goggles, long-sleeved clothing and sturdy shoes in case stray shards of glass fall. Then, follow these steps:

1. Place a towel or sheet below the window to collect the broken glass.

2. With your thick gloves, carefully lift or punch out the large pieces, and break them into smaller pieces on the linen.

3. With a hammer and a chisel, pound out all the remaining glass from the frame.

4. Screw a large piece of plywood into the window frame until the pane can be replaced.

5. Discard the broken glass in a cardboard box. Don't throw it in a plastic garbage bag, unless you want your cantaloupe seeds and fast food wrappers to spill all over the driveway as you take out the trash.

How To Deal with "Lazy Landlord Syndrome"

No matter how you treat your apartment, something is bound to break at one time or another. If you have a lazy landlord, it may take several weeks before someone comes to fix your showerhead or microwave. In the meantime, you can try these troubleshooting tips to repair basic home utilities and appliances. Remember, when in doubt, call the repairman!

Gas

It is illegal and dangerous to even attempt to open, fix, or improve your gas lines or pipes. For these services, call someone from your gas company. If you ever smell an unusual amount of gas or suspect a gas leak, go to your gas meter and turn it off. Get to fresh air immediately and call a serviceman.

Electricity

Don't attempt electrical repairs that are beyond your level of expertise. But, if your power ever goes out in a room, and you do not think it is due to a widespread power outage, first check to see if the circuit is overloaded. That happens when too many hair dryers and curling irons are being used at once. If this isn't the problem, go to your breaker box. Turn off the breakers for the desired outlet, then turn them on again. If the power still doesn't return, consult an electrician. Never stick metal objects in outlets and keep all forms of electricity away from water.

Clogged Drains

This is a common problem you will surely encounter sometime in your life. To unclog your drain, first pull the drain stopper out or up as far as possible and check for hair or other debris. (Now there's a *Fear Factor* food challenge.) Remove it with a long thin device, like a screwdriver. You can also try using the suction of a toilet plunger to unclog the drain. If that doesn't work, try using a chemical cleaner like Drano. If it remains clogged, you will need to get a snake (no, not a boa, but a metal device plumbers use) to fish down the drain and unclog it.

Toilet Problems

Agh! Your roommates will be home any minute and "somehow" your toilet got clogged while you were home. Don't call the plumber just yet. If your toilet is clogged, you should first put on gloves and remove any abnormal blockage in whatever way you deem most sanitary. Then, get a plunger, lower it into the toilet water at an angle, and place it over the entire drain hole in the base of the toilet bowl. Forming a suction over the hole, pump the plunger up and down until you hear the toilet start to flush.

For a toilet that runs, lift up the lid on the back of the toilet and check for the following: a cracked or overflowing tube, a waterlogged float ball, a float arm that does not rise high enough, or a chain that has become disconnected. You can try to stop the running by reconnecting the chain, replacing the ball or tube, or bending the float arm down. If your toilet is leaking water—or other nasty liquids—try tightening the bolts in the tank or resealing the bowl to the base. Any other toilet problems are best left to a plumber.

Garbage Disposal

If your disposal ever makes a strange noise, turn it off, wait a few minutes, and carefully remove any metal or foreign objects that might be stuck in it. If your disposal makes a loud, steady noise or stops working, it has probably jammed. Turn it off and let it rest for a few minutes. Then, press the reset button on the motor (which is most likely located under the sink). If it still doesn't work, see if you can unjam it from below the motor by turning the flywheel with a small Allen wrench.

Dishwasher

If your dishwasher will not run, double check the settings, and make sure the door is locked. If you have a more complex problem like a broken door latch or faulty wires, consult with a professional. If the problem is that your dishes are not getting clean enough, make sure you are using the right type of detergent for your model, the water is hot enough, the dishes are stacked correctly and not blocking the spray arms, and that the detergent dispenser opens when the cycle starts. If applicable, using Jet-Dry in the proper dispenser monthly can also add sparkle to those spoons and salad plates!

Refrigerator

If your refrigerator stops running correctly, first check the electrical cord and make sure it is in good shape and plugged in correctly. If it is not cooling properly, check the coolant dial and make sure it is turned to the recommended temperature level. Other problems that may cause the refrigerator to stop running or not cool properly are dirty or broken condenser coils, broken compressors or thermostats, or a door that is not working correctly. If you couldn't care less about learning what a condenser coil or a compressor is, and you just want cold milk, call Sears!

Okay, Fix-it Friends, now you can spend all of your security deposit refund on a new HDTV! Let's just hope it works . . .

chapter 10

How to Keep Bleeding and Shrinking
Out of the Laundromat

How clean are your clothes?

1. The last thing I used bleach for was _____.
   a. My bathtub
   b. My hair
   c. My white button-down

2. An ironing board is a good place to _____.
   a. Throw your clothes at the end of a day
   b. Stack newspapers
   c. Iron—duh

3. Red socks and white socks:
   a. Make for an interesting fashion trend
   b. Who owns red socks?
   c. Should *never* be washed together!

If you scored:

Mostly a's: Stained
Mostly b's: Stone-washed
Mostly c's: You have three stain sticks!?!

If words like "Maytag," "Clorox," and "Tide" are foreign to you, it's your roommates' lucky day! They will love you for reading a brief instructional on how to make your odor more pleasant. Laundry is something that everyone should do at least once a month, although most people opt for a weekly visit to the washing machine.

To get started, you're going to need some supplies. Minimalists will be able to get by with some form of a hamper or laundry bag and detergent. But for those of you who want to lengthen the lifespan of your clothes while maintaining a respectable appearance, you'll need these as well: bleach, stain or spot remover, dryer sheets, an iron, spray bottle and ironing board (or kitchen table protected with a towel). When your hamper is full (or you're tired of wearing the same black t-shirt everyday), make your way to the nearest washing machine, armed with your laundry-doing supplies and this book.

Laundry 101

Just as your washing machine goes through cycles, so does the laundry-doing process. Follow these steps.

1 **Read the tag.** Every item of clothing is accompanied with a little tag geared toward enlightening the 20/20 reader on how to get maximum cleansing results. Obeying these orders will keep your whites white and your colors bright. Always read the tag, because some clothes come with the instructions "dry clean only," "hand wash," or "line dry."

For dry clean only items (which are usually made out of silk, wool, leather, suede, velvet, or some other expensive fabric), go to your nearest or cheapest dry cleaner. Because I know a twenty-year-old who is scared to go to the dry cleaner, here's how it works. When you drop the item off, they will give you an identification tag and tell you to return in a couple of days. When you return (with your tag), your garment should look better than when you bought it. Always inspect the item before you pay for the service, because they will offer nothing more than a shoulder shrug if it takes you a couple of weeks to discover that their machines ate your buttons and ripped out your hem.

Dry cleaning can be expensive. If you simply want a collared shirt cleaned and ironed, it shouldn't cost you more than $2. But to get dresses, suits, sweaters, and other items cleaned, it can cost anywhere from $3 to $15. So, don't eat mustard while wearing cashmere.

"Hand wash" means simply that. Fill your sink halfway full with warm water and pour in a little Woolite. If your ancestors passed down one of those old-fashioned scrub boards, by all means use that for posterity's sake, but I'm guessing you don't have one. So simply give the item of clothing a massage until it is clean.

I am also going to assume that your backyard does not feature a clothes line or grazing goat. Thus, you will need to be creative with the term "line dry." I usually hang wet items with this instruction over a chair or door. Just be careful, because sometimes a wet item molds to the shape it was dried in, and you might end up with some darts and seams in places they just don't naturally belong. To avoid this, hang the wet item on a plastic hanger on your shower or curtain rod until it is dry.

2 **Stain removal.** Argh, don't you hate it when chocolate sauce drips down your new white sweater? As colorful as that can be, there are ways to get it out—if you act fast. Whenever you are dealing with a major stain on something you would like to wear again, treat it as quickly as possible. Now's the time to pull out one of those dandy Tide stain sticks they sell by the gum at the check-out. Or dab at the stain with a moistened cloth, but don't rub it in. When you get home, either apply a stain removal product, or soak it in a little color-safe Clorox bleach mixed with water. Then, wash

the stained garment in the hottest water recommended on the tag as soon as possible. Never machine dry or iron a stained product until you've tried everything possible to get it clean, because heat will set the stain. Here are some extra-tough, yet common stains and suggested ways to remove them:

- **Ink.** Apply stain remover, hair spray or rubbing alcohol. Rub on detergent and wash.

- **Blood.** Rinse with cold water. If you have meat tenderizer, apply it to the area and let it soak. If not, wash with powdered detergent ASAP.

- **Makeup and fruit juices.** Pour boiling water over the stain and rub a bar of soap on it.

- **Grass, grease, mud, and carbonated drinks.** Rub stain with detergent and soak in warm water. If stain remains, try soaking in rubbing alcohol and water.

- **Dye that bleeds.** To prevent this, wash multi-colored items at a cold temperature, and remove them from the washer as soon as the rinse cycle completes. Rub a stain remover on the affected area and rewash right away.

- **Alcohol, coffee, sweat, and deodorant.** Soak the area in a mixture of white vinegar and warm water, then wash.

3 **Wash cycle.** You may need to prepare in advance by having quarters or a swipe card ready to work the machines at your laundromat. Once you are ready, separate your clothes into piles based on their colors, and sometimes fabrics. It's best to wash towels separately, as they tend to produce a large amount of lint. You will want to separate your colors into three piles: whites, lights, and darks. I must admit I usually do just two loads—whites/light pastels and bright/dark colors. But, if you do this, never wash a new colored item with something in a different shade or you may wind up with some painful bleeding.

Select the appropriate water temperature for the load you are washing. Wash whites in hot water; but when washing colors, stick to warm or cold temperatures to minimize fading and bleeding. Read the directions on the machine, but most washers will say to put one scoop of detergent in, then turn the water on and let the machine fill while you add the clothing. For white clothing, you can add some liquid bleach to the bleach dispenser, but never add a bleach product to colored clothes unless the bleach specifically says it is color safe! Avoid overloading the machine, and set the water level high enough so the clothes will have enough room to circulate and the machine will drain properly. Wash cycles normally take about thirty to forty minutes.

4 **Drying.** Once your clothes are clean, dry them as soon as possible to minimize mildew and wrinkling. After you have cleaned out the lint filter, load (but don't overload) the dryer with your clothes. Adding a dryer sheet or fabric softener will prevent static and will leave your clothes more fluffy and pleasant smelling, just like the Snuggle bear promises. Select a temperature, keeping in mind that the hotter the heat, the more it shrinks. Then, turn it on.

Dryers can take anywhere from one to two hours to dry your clothes. If you are using a community laundry facility, check on your clothes to make sure people don't steal or dump them. Once when I was in college, I threw a load in, went out for the evening, and came back to find my underwear and other freshly cleaned clothes thrown on the dirty floor. There are people who will do this if they are tired of waiting for a machine!

Once dry, fold your clothes as soon as you can to minimize wrinkling. Remember to check the tags—some items (including anything plastic or wool) are not meant to be machine dried!

5 **Iron!** This last step is one of the most annoying parts of not having Mom down the hall. Ironing is

a very tedious, time-consuming task, yet it makes a world of difference in your presentation. Like drying, some things are not meant to be ironed; instead, you will need to steam them (a pain) or have them professionally steamed (expensive). Sometimes hanging the garment in a sauna-like atmosphere (like your bathroom during a hot shower) will steam the wrinkles out. But, if not, crank out that old ironing board and a spray bottle.

Preheat the iron to the designated temperature for the fabric. When in doubt, start with the lowest heat. Never apply an iron to anything plastic or synthetic, or you may end up with a burning smell that will linger for days. And amateurs, you may want to iron your clothing turned inside out until you figure it out. Spray the surface with water. Move the iron across the garment in slow circles, but never leave the iron on one spot for more than five seconds, unless you have a thing for brown triangles.

Those aiming for that sharp, military look may want to use a spray starch. Spray and iron each section of the shirt separately, starting with the sleeves and the collar, then moving to the back and then to the front two flaps. For slacks, iron each leg with the seam in the middle of the ironing board's surface so that your creases will run down the front of your leg. If just thinking about this gives you headache, do what I do—buy wrinkle-free fabrics and a wrinkle spray and call it a day!

This chapter was written for all of you who lug a duffel bag of dirty clothes home every other weekend. Trust me, once you get the hang of it, doing laundry is not the worst thing in the world. Your parents will thank you.

chapter 11

Getting "Customer Service, May I Help You?" to Help You

Do you get what you want on the phone?

1. The Better Business Bureau _____.
   a. Sounds vaguely familiar
   b. Maintains ethical business practices
   c. Is number three on my speed dial

2. Telemarketers are _____.
   a. All around me—I'm at work right now
   b. Great dinner companions
   c. Annoying!

3. If your new surround sound arrived broken, who would hear about it?
   a. My roommates
   b. The manufacturer's complaints department
   c. The C.E.O. of Samsung

If you scored:

Mostly a's: Nope.
Mostly b's: Maybe you're better in person.
Mostly c's: You get what you want everywhere.

The average teen spends more than enough time on the phone texting, Twittering, and ordering take-out. When you enter the Real World, you will still spend a decent amount of time on the phone, but a large portion of it will be "taking care of business." In an adult's life, many situations are taken care of by phone. You may need to schedule an appointment with an auto shop, a refrigerator repairman, a dentist, or a hair salon. Your sink is leaking, your newspaper isn't being delivered properly, or maybe your surround sound did arrive broken (we must have the same luck)! Your success in getting what you want out of these phone calls depends on two things—how whacked the person on the other end of the phone is, and how well you handle the situation.

When dealing with customer service representatives, there are six steps you can follow that almost ensure that things will go your way.

1 **Have a clear understanding** of what the problem is and how you want it fixed. For instance, know your schedule if you need to set up an appointment. Know exactly what is broken if you need a repair.

2 **Become the phone rep's "friend."** Are you nicer to your friends than you are to strangers? Of course. To reach the status of the phone operator's "friend," start the call with the words, "Hello, how are you doing today?" Use a friendly tone and make small talk when the situation allows. Call the person by name, once you learn it. Be the breath of fresh air that is so rare for people who work in cubicles and wear headsets all day. I guarantee this trick works!

3 **But if it doesn't, take it to the top!** Make sure you are talking to the right person. If the person who answers the phone does not seem apt or able to give you what you want, ask to speak to his supervisor. Don't waste time complaining to someone who can't help you. The more you escalate the situation, the more powerful the person is with whom you'll speak, and the better your chance of getting what you want.

4 **Use flattery.** Which comment would make you more willing to lend a shirt to your roommate: "Hey, let me borrow that shirt" or, "You have the coolest clothes—I wish I dressed as well as you. Do you think I could maybe borrow that shirt sometime?" The same goes for customer service. Try these phrases: "I know your company exudes professionalism and wants nothing more than for your customers to be pleased with your products, but . . ." and "You are the repair shop I recommend to all of my friends, and I know you must be so busy, but seeing as my (product) really needs to be serviced soon, I was wondering if you could squeeze me in?" A little flattery never hurts.

5 **Practice "justified disappointment" rather than "flippant anger."** Do not swear, yell, or violently threaten someone on the phone. It will only make you sound ignorant, and it will immediately cause the person on the other end to become defensive. It is okay to be upset, but a controlled, firm voice goes a lot further than a flailing one.

6 **Keep written documentation of all phone contacts.** The company you are talking to most likely notes in their database every time you call with a complaint. Thus, it will seem very professional to them if you have done the same. For every contact made, write down the date, time, person with whom you spoke, and what was said. That way, you can specifically cite what was promised and by whom. The company will react to you much more positively if you state the facts.

7 **Casually mention "the law."** In escalating your problem, casually mention "the law" as a last resort, if you feel you are still being taken advantage of by a company or service provider. It never hurts to throw in the fact that your lawyer agrees that you have been wronged. Corporations do not want to waste their time fighting off piddling law suits, so the mere mention of having or knowing a lawyer may do the trick.

I have followed these steps numerous times and gotten what I wanted from corporations. Here is one example. You know all those companies that send you flyers stating that you can buy six books/CD's/lampshades for one dollar if you join their club? (Never join one of those!) Well, somehow, a book company thought that by my agreement to accept a free gift that was advertised as a "no-obligation gift to you," that I then wanted them to send me two books a month along with a hefty bill for the rest of my life, or until the end of time, or whichever came last. Here is how I took care of it:

Customer Service Rep: Hello, _____ Books, how may I help you?

Me: Yes, hello, how are you doing today?

CSR (startled): Fine . . . Thanks—uh, what can I do for you?

Me: Well, I agreed to accept a free gift with "no obligations," yet I have now found myself trapped into receiving two books a month that I am required to pay for or send back, at my expense. I see how your company is great for people who have the time and money to read two hardback books a month, but seeing as I am a poor college student, I would like very much not to be a member of your organization, please.

CSR: Well, if you would have bought a magnifying glass (maybe she didn't really say that) and read the small print on the offer, you would have seen that by accepting the free gift, you are agreeing to join our club and that entails receiving a monthly offer until you have purchased at least four books at regular price, plus shipping and handling, and then you can cancel at any time.

Me: So you are saying that the only way I can get out of your club is by buying four books at $22.95 each, plus $17.95 shipping and handling, and then I am free to go?

CSR: That would be correct.

Me: Well, then, can I please speak to your supervisor?

CSR: Hold, please.

Then, twenty minutes of Barbara Streisand. Luckily it's a 1-800 number.

Supervisor: How may I help you? *(The above conversation repeats in its entirety, including the part where I ask to speak to the supervisor's supervisor.)*

Supervisor's Supervisor: Hello, yes, our customer service representatives have filled me in on your problem. I'm sorry, but by accepting the free gift, you are now enrolled in our club.

Me: I understand that you feel that way. The problem is, I always thought of your company as highly reputable and not one that is prone to fine-print obligations. In fact, my lawyer feels the same way, and he said it's about time someone did something about "clubs" like yours. I would hate to waste anyone's time going to court with such a trivial matter. I was hoping you could just take my name off your list, as I truly did not realize that by accepting a "free gift," I would be so indebted to you.

SS: Well, if you were honestly mistaken, I suppose we can remove your name from our membership, but let's not let this happen again.

Me: You got it, boss.

I've learned when you are a justifiably dissatisfied yet rational consumer, you can work your way up through the channels of a corporation's customer service circuit. The $7 per hour employees do not want to deal with you, so they'll gladly let you speak to the manager, supervisor, district manager, corporate supervisor. Then whoever the "head" is gets on the phone.

But sometimes, things still don't go your way, in which case, you have one more option: the Better Business Bureau. They are the respected source for checking into a business's integrity, and most companies have customer service department procedures in place just so they can stay off the BBB's bad list. So if you're still miffed, give them a call.

How to Deal with Telemarketers

You will inevitably one day be contacted by a telemarketer who will not be able to pronounce your name even if it is John Smith. In fact, you will probably one day be a professional annoyance for a momentary time as you put yourself through college. So remember, the annoying person trying to get you to switch to MCI or apply for a Discover card is a lot like you. So, put away your whistle or cowbell and be somewhat patient. But, if you have placed your number with the "Do Not Call Registry" and are still receiving way too many dinnertime calls, remember these tricks:

- Simply say, "We don't accept calls from solicitors," or "I am heading out the door, sorry" and hang up.

- Say "No, No, No." And no, you are not scolding the person, but most telemarketers are trained to not give up on someone until the person says "no" three times.

- Reply, "I am currently eating breakfast/lunch/dinner at home with my family, but I would love to talk to you. What time will you be home eating with your family and what is your home phone number, so I can call you back then?"

- Ask to be taken off the company's calling list—if you

are officially taken off the list (they will confirm your name and address and send you a confirmation letter), in most states you are legally entitled to punitive damages for harassment, if they should call you back.

May all of your calls get you what you want. If not, give me a call. What? What's that? I can't hear you. We must have a bad connection! Um, I'll call you back later . . .

chapter 12

On the Road Again

How soon will you be back on the road?

1. A carburetor is _____.
    a. An alligator that lives under cars
    b. That button by the radio?
    c. A device in which air and gasoline create an explosive mixture in a combustion engine

2. To jump start a dead battery, you will need _____.
    a. A jump rope
    b. Daddy
    c. Jumper cables and another car's running battery

3. You should get a 30,000 checkup _____.
    a. If your car costs $30,000
    b. The 30,000th time you drive your car
    c. When your odometer hits 30,000 miles

If you scored:

Mostly a's: Try releasing your parking break.
Mostly b's: Just call AAA.
Mostly c's: You're already there.

Your high school status was probably influenced by the four-wheeled machine you hauled into the parking lot. I'm sorry to tell you (or pleased if you drove a Gremlin) that for the most part, the Real World is not that shallow. Cars become liabilities as you have to balance car payments with auto insurance, gas bills, oil changes, car washes, and regular maintenance. Once you are footing the bill, you will care a lot more about how to take good care of your heap of metal, and a lot less about what make or model is.

Now some of you girls might be thinking, "I don't want to read a boring chapter about cars." I don't blame you. And some of you guys are probably thinking, "Like I'm going to listen to a chick talk about cars!" I don't blame you, either. Well, I have hung around enough automobile-savvy people to figure out a few basic things about how a car works, simple auto maintenance habits, and how to stay safe on the road. And, for those of you who are still not entirely interested in learning about wiper blades and roadside assistance, if you keep your motor running, I'll throw in some tricks that will get you out of speeding tickets—not that you'll ever need to know that.

How A Car Works

In case you're going on Jeopardy and wanted to know what happens after you put the key in the ignition, here you go. (To make this more exciting, hold your breath like you're driving though a tunnel—and read fast.)

When you crank the ignition, a battery current charges the electric starting motor. This turns the crankshaft in the engine and starts to move the pistons and rods. At the same time, the car's fuel pump starts pumping fuel from the gas tank into the engine. Sparks of electricity ignite the fuel, and the engine starts—all in just a few seconds.

Once the engine starts, it maintains the power. Then, the

gears in the transmission carry the power to the car's wheels, making it possible for the car to move. There are four or five sets of gears in cars that control the power and direction of an engine's force. Cars with automatic transmissions shift through the gears automatically; manual transmissions require you to press a clutch and move a shifting rod to change from gear to gear. First gear and reverse are the most powerful gears, as they get the car moving, while the other gears maintain a car's movement. When you apply your foot to the brakes, the brakes use friction to slow down the wheels. A parking brake connects to the brakes but acts as its own system. Its primary job is to keep the car from moving when parked. And now, you're ready to roll. Whew, exhale!

Simple Car Maintenance

Be good to your car, and it will most likely be good to you. Following are a few simple tips to keep your car in optimal driving condition.

Fuel

There are different grades of gasoline you can fill your car with; most stations offer 87, 89, 91, and diesel. Check your owner's manual to make sure you are using the right kind of gasoline for your car. You should always try to keep your gas tank half-full, or at the least a quarter full. Not only will this keep you from running out of gas, but it will prevent your fuel pump from overheating (because the gasoline cools the tank) and from becoming contaminated from sediments in the tank.

Oil Changes

The standard rule for getting your oil changed has always been to do it every 3,000 miles or three months; but some cars can go almost twice that, so again, check your manual. At least once a month, you should check the level of your oil, because having to buy a new engine is not fun or cheap, and that's what you will have to do if you have an unattended oil leak. To check your oil, pull out the dipstick of the oil filter, wipe it clean, and then stick it into the filter and pull it out again to see if it is at the suggested safe level. I could also throw in a little how-to on changing your own oil, but by the time it would take to read it, you could have been to Jiffylube and back.

Wiper Blades

Your windshield wipers are not just there for cosmetic reasons. They are a safety feature, as they provide you with a clear view when driving. So, unless you like driving in the rain with your head stuck out the window (been there, done that), clean and replace your blades as needed. If your windshield is still dirty after using your windshield washer, clean the blades with a rag soaked in a mild detergent, then rinse with water. If it is still not clean, replace the blades either professionally or by yourself. To do it yourself, pull the wiper arm out away from your windshield and remove the old blade by pushing the lock pin and pulling it out. Slide the new blade onto the wiper arm until you hear it click. You can buy blades at auto parts stores and even at some gas stations.

Fluids

There are seven standard fluids under every car's hood that should be checked during your oil change: engine coolant level (antifreeze mixed with water), window washer level, brake fluid, power steering fluid, transmission fluid, differential fluid, and battery water. Make sure these are topped off regularly, or do it yourself by following the instructions in your owner's manual.

Tires

Just like a dinner is only as good as its dessert, a car is only as good as its tires! If they are flat, you're immobile. So, keep a tire pressure gauge in your glove compartment, and check the level of each tire when your car feels lopsided. Just kidding, do it way before that. You can fill flat tires for free, thanks to a dandy law that keeps us all properly inflated, by visiting the air pump at any service station. To pump it up, just unscrew the cap on your tire, place the air pump completely over the hole, and fill until the machine tells you the tire is at its preferred pressure (again, in your manual).

Always keep a spare tire and jacking tools (a jack, tire blocks and wheel nut wrench), in your car. If you ever have a blowout in L.A. rush-hour traffic, going seventy mph, you can change your own tire by following these basic steps. But always check the directions included with your jacking tools, as well.

1. Pull your car over to a safe place on the side of the road, pop your hood, and turn on your hazard lights to warn other drivers of your presence. Make sure everyone gets out of your car.

2. Park on level ground, and pull the parking brake. If you have a manual transmission, shift into reverse. Turn the car off.

3. Block the wheel that is diagonally opposite from the flat wheel with tire blocks, large bricks or rocks to prevent it from moving.

4. Align the jack between the jack-up notches on your car by your tire, and fit the groove of the jack head between the notches. Raise the jack until the car is clearly off the ground.

5. Use your wheel nut wrench to loosen each wheel nut by turning them counterclockwise. When all are removed, take off the tire.

6. Clean any dirt from the surface, then put the new tire on and tighten each wheel nut with your hand until it is tight.

7. Use the wrench to tighten the nuts even more; then lower the car to the ground slowly. Once on the ground, use the wrench to tighten each wheel nut one final time. Then, you're good to go!

Battery

Cars have a big fat battery in them that just keeps going, as long as you don't leave your lights or radio on when the car is off. The battery recharges itself when your car is running because it is connected to the alternator, which generates electrical currents that flow back to the battery. But, if you do one day accidentally leave a door cracked open for a bit too long, you are going to need jumper cables and a helping hand (preferably one with a working car). Park your cars facing each other in a safe place, and pop your hoods. Turn your cars off, and then follow these steps exactly, to avoid a nice little electrical jolt:

1. Connect the red cables to the positive (+) posts on each battery.

2. Connect the black cable to the negative (-) post of the charged battery.

3. Connect the other end of the black cable to an unpainted part on the engine block, as far away as possible from the battery.

4. Start the car with the good battery and let it idle for a few minutes before attempting to start the disabled vehicle.

5. Remove cables in reverse order.

Car Wash

If you want your car to play any sort of a role in your social life, you will need to keep it looking like something your friends won't be embarrassed to be seen in. The easiest way to do this is to pay someone else to do it (I see a theme here), but it is more cost effective to wash it yourself—unless you use hydrogen peroxide. If you live in an area with a lot of pollution, acid rain, or salt, you will need to wash your car once a week. Otherwise, give it a good scrub at least once a month. The el cheapo way to do this is to fill a bucket with warm water and a little dish soap, grab a rag, and borrow your neighbor's hose; but doing it this way could take off your polish and make your neighbor mad. A better way is to buy car washing products specifically designed to clean your car's body, windows, tires, chrome and aluminum, and interior.

For the body of your car, use a sponge or towel that is clean and won't be abrasive to your car. It is best to wash your car in the shade so the soap doesn't dry before you can rinse it. First, divide your car into sections. Starting at the top of your car, rinse each section with a water hose, then scrub it with the soapy cloth. Finish each section by rinsing off the soap suds, then towel dry. Don't forget to clean underneath your vehicle. If you want a nice smooth shine, apply wax, following the directions on the bottle. Then, scrub your tires and rims with a cleaner and brush designed for them. And don't forget the inside—wash your windows with a glass cleaner and a dry cloth. If your car has tinted windows, use soapy water instead of glass cleaner, because the ammonia in most glass cleaners can harm the tint. Wipe the dash, door panels, and controls with a rag dampened with an interior cleaner. Finally, vacuum the entire interior, and use a fabric cleaner to remove any spots. Then, go joyriding!

Check-Ups

Just like you, your car needs regular check-ups to maintain its physical and emotional health after you drive it to the ground. If you haven't figured it out by now, you should consult your owner's manual to see what services your car requires to remain in optimal shape.

Most cars require visits to a professional auto shop for a tune-up every 15,000 miles. Make these visits a priority so that all the plugs, fluids, and filters are checked out. You will also want to have your tires rotated, belts replaced, and electrical board examined on schedule. And how do you know which car doctor is right for you?

A good mechanic is a friend for life. So, once you find one you can trust, make sure you bring him cookies and invite him to your brother's wedding to keep him in your inner circle. When you move to a new area, ask around and see which auto shops your neighbors like, or consult with your local Car Care Council Certified Inspection Center, AAA, or ASE to see whom they recommend. It is better to have a good mechanic than a cheap mechanic. You get what you pay for, and if you don't believe me, watch all those Dateline and 20/20 specials featuring "auto mechanic rip-offs."

Auto Safety

Most accidents are caused by someone being stupid. So to avoid clanging metal, crumpled fenders, and dealing with insurance companies, memorize these guidelines, and repeat them to yourself three times each morning before you get in your car.

- Always wear a seatbelt. Always. And wear them how they are designed, with your shoulder strap in front, and your seat upright.

- Never drink and drive. Pick a designated driver before you go out.

- Only drive if you are licensed and insured.

- Don't let other people drive your car. I learned this the hard way: when my friend wrecked my car, it stayed on my insurance record for several years!

- Keep your doors locked as you drive to avoid carjacking.

- Be a defensive driver and avoid road rage. Plowing down someone's dog because they tailgated you is just not very mature behavior.

- Join AAA. It is definitely worth the annual membership fee. You get free towing and roadside assistance, within reason. Call 1-800-AAA-HELP to join.

- Driving is a privilege, not a right. Always obey traffic rules.

- Never try to beat a train—never.

- Keep a car safety kit with you, with a flashlight, blanket jumper cables, first aid kit, emergency gas carrier, jacking tools, flares, and a charged cell phone. The law requires cell phone companies to allow all phones to call 911, even if the phone is not part of a service contract, so always keep a phone and car charger with you.

- Consider installing a car alarm or some other type of security device.

- Talking on cell phones, changing music, lighting cigarettes, eating, applying makeup, and engaging in emotionally charged conversations with fellow passengers are driving distractions and cause many accidents and deaths each year.

• Don't be a distracted driver—pay attention to the road!

Uh-Oh! What Was That?

Regardless of how much your car is worth, or how recently it was serviced, there are always nails, stray cows, and bad luck on the road. If you find yourself in any of these predicaments, carefully follow these procedures:

• **You have a tire blow-out.** Take your foot off the gas, and apply even pressure to the brake. Firmly grip your steering wheel and pull your car off the road to safety. Change your tire, or call AAA (if you are a member).

• **Your brakes go out.** Turn on your hazard lights. Take your foot off the gas, and try pumping your brakes several times. Downshift or try to go uphill to lose speed. Gently pull and release your parking brake to slow down. Pull to the side of the road and get help.

• **Your lights go out.** Try driving in a straight line to the side of the road. Turn on your hazard lights, if they are working, and check your fuses. Get help.

• **Your steering fails.** Evenly brake to slow down. Turn on your hazards and honk your horn to get attention. Pull the car to safety, and call AAA.

• **Your car catches on fire.** Immediately pull your car away from the road and get all passengers out. Call 911. From a distance, extinguish the fire, if possible. If the fire is near the gas tank, run, because you need to stay 500 feet away from the car.

- **You hear a strange noise or smell an unusual odor from your car.** Stop the car immediately on the side of the road, and get out. If there is no smoke coming from under the hood, lift the hood, and check your fluids and oil. If you are uncertain what the problem is, call for help.

- **You get in an accident.** Never drive away—you could be charged with a hit-and-run, even if it wasn't your fault. It is a good idea to keep a disposable camera in your glove box for proof of liability in an accident. If the accident was a minor fender-bender, pull your cars to safety. Try to get a witness to pull over, too—especially if it was not your fault. Call the police, and while you are waiting, exchange information. Ask to see the person's driver's license and insurance card, and make sure you get his name, phone number, address, driver's license number, insurance company's name, policy number, phone number, and address. File a report with the police, and follow up with your insurance companies.

- **You hear a siren behind you.** If the siren is a speeding emergency vehicle that is not in pursuit of you, immediately—but safely—slow down and pull to the right side of the road. It is extremely tacky to chase an ambulance (although lawyers do it all the time).

If a police officer is signaling for you to pull over, do so in a safe spot. To make the ticket-receiving experience less painful, do not argue with the officer or tell him how mad you are that you forgot to turn on your radar detector. Make sure you know what you are being ticketed for before you sign the citation. You will have to contest the ticket or pay it within a few weeks—don't forget to do that, or a warrant will be issued for your arrest! I know that crying and flirting sometimes get people out of tickets, but they're stale tactics. Not that I would ever tell you to lie to an officer to be excused from a ticket, but I have "heard" these following methods work in contesting speeding tickets.

- Girls, a "feminine emergency" will prompt most male officers to let you go, even if you were going 24 mph over the speed limit in a thunderstorm. (Don't ask how I know that.)

- Sudden, sharp pains and episodes relating to diseases and pregnancies can cause temporary insanity, don't you think?

- *Tommy Boy's* "bee scare" was effective—if some sort of terrifying insect was harassing you, how could you be focusing on your speed?

- "Officer, I am so glad you pulled me over—I was totally freaked out, because some guy with a gun in a big, black truck was chasing me and I was just trying to get away from him. But you saved me! Oh, look, there he goes!"

- An employee of an insurance company told me that if the processing of a ticket is never completed, it will never go on your insurance record. So, overpay your ticket by $1, and when the DMV sends you a check for $1, don't cash it.

- Invest in Prepaid Legal Services. For about $25 a month, you are guaranteed a standby lawyer (for no additional cost), whenever you want one. If there is one thing traffic judges hate more than speeders in their courtrooms, it's lawyers. Lawyers can always find something unjust about your citation, and their mere appearance will cut your ticket in half.

So, buckle up and start your engines. It's time to get back on the road again!

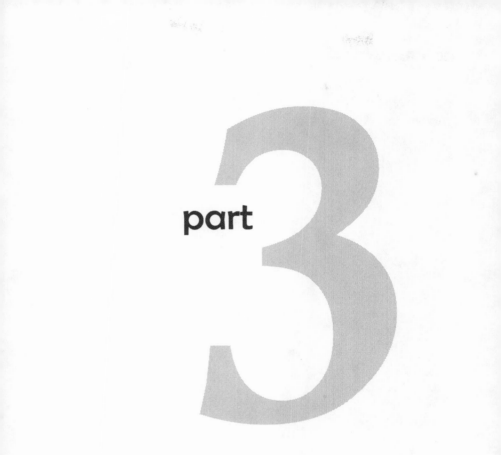

part **3**

Surviving Financially

chapter 13

How to Get, Keep, and Quit a Job

Who would hire you?

1. Unless otherwise directed, what should you
    wear to a job interview?
    a. Whatever's clean
    b. Whatever you feel comfortable in
    c. Professional attire—suits, ties, and dresses

2. A headhunter is a _____.
    a. Cannibal
    b. Military operation
    c. Corporate recruiter

3. If you get "axed," then you've been _____.
    a. Killed
    b. In the logging industry
    c. Fired

If you scored:

Mostly a's: Payless Shoe Source
Mostly b's: Footlocker
Mostly c's: Jimmy Choo

Your childhood mind probably entertained the occasional thought, "When I grow up, I want to be a (fill in the blank with something that pays a lot and makes you really famous)." Real American boys surely dreamed about being pro baseball players. And little girls twinkled and twirled as they dreamed of becoming ballerinas. As kids grow older, idealists hold on to their dreams, while realists change their career goals to exciting fields like teaching and sales. Well, depending on how hard you work and how committed you are, you may have the opportunity to hit the big leagues or take center stage. And in the meantime, as you work your way through school, you will need a little something to keep the bills paid. So, as you are now again asking yourself "What do I want to be when I really grow up?" consider using the following resources to help you get a job. Just remember that the job market is a lot like a baseball game—only coed.

Minor Leagues

If you are not a trust fund kid, you will need another way to fund $10 movie tickets, your Nordy's bill, and your Starbucks addiction. Most amateur job seekers consider fields like telemarketing, child care, food service, retail, and the great outdoors as the way to pay the bills. My first real job was a lifeguard position at my town's indoor community pool. Because the place was indoors, most of the patrons were wearing swim team Speedos or over 89, so I frequently fought the Sandman sitting up in my big, tall, power-trippy lifeguard chair. It paid fifty cents an hour more than minimum wage, and was a completely not-glamorous job, but it did add to my experience when I applied to be a lifeguard at a swank country club pool the next summer. You never know where your little positions may lead you—even if all you get out of them is a free dip in a salty hot tub and a somewhat decent reference on your resume. To find a minor league job, here are some places you can look:

- Most schools, colleges, and community centers have a job board with listings of local places of employment that are hiring.

- Gas stations, grocery stores, and newsstands offer free "Employment Guides" that list many occupations the average Joe can handle.

- Your local newspaper has a daily or weekly Classified section with listings of hiring companies.

- Where do you deplete your funds? The mall? Movies? McDonald's? Guess what—people work there. And you can, too. Just respectfully ask the manager for a job application, and you may get discounts or freebies of your favorite things, as well as a paycheck.

Once you find a job that is somewhat appealing, call or visit the company, and ask for application information. Since the required experience and list of responsibilities isn't too complex for these standard jobs, you shouldn't have too hard of a time getting hired, unless there is a warrant out for your arrest. But, if you have already folded pocket tees at the Gap for three years, you may be ready for the . . .

Major Leagues

The words "executive" and "professional" usually accompany job descriptions in the big time working world. These jobs require some type of degree, formal training, or scanned and altered diploma you swiped off the Internet (I'm not suggesting you try this). People who work in the major leagues don't talk about their "jobs"; rather, they call them their "careers" or "occupations." Jobs, or excuse me, occupations such as these include those in the fields of medicine, law, technology, education, real estate, and anything that has the word "incorporated" after the name of the company. Major league professions require major job-hunting skills. Following are some ideas:

- If you are a senior at a college, university, or trade school, check with the employment department for the list of companies who regularly recruit at that school. Attend any seminars or interview opportunities those companies have scheduled.

- Attend school or community career fairs, at which businesses set up booths and send professional shpiel-givers to tell you why their company is number one at so-and-so, for two years in a row! Request application information there, and keep the business cards of everyone you talk to.

- Connections, connections. My dad once told me, "It's not what you know, it's who you know." At first, I refused to believe such superficial blabber—until I learned it was true. Think of every kid you know who was given a luxury vehicle for the big sixteenth, and get in tight with the fam. Employees of a company get applicants interviews a lot more often than applications do. Always try to network with the people you meet, and remember to keep their names and contact information filed at the front of your brain.

- Become best buds with a headhunter. These people are contracted with companies who are hiring to find qualified people to fill job openings. You can find headhunters targeted for your field by googling "Executive Search Consultants," or you can use an online headhunting source like *www.headhunter.net*. While a headhunter isn't directly hiring you, she still doesn't want to deal with unprofessional people, so tell the recruiter exactly what type of job you are looking for, and present her with an up-to-date, polished resume and the salary range you are seeking. The recruiter will submit this information only to the companies she feels you are qualified for (to maintain her reputation), so don't harass her if you do not have a job interview every afternoon.

• Post your resume online! Try a job-seeking site like Monster.com, or just enter "Job Search" and do a key word search for the career you are pursuing.

Once you've targeted what type of job you want, put on an extra layer of deodorant, because it's time for...

Tryouts

In the job application process, you will hopefully gain two things: interviewing experience and—a job! To maximize the success of your "tryouts," carefully consider these two factors:

First, is the job right for me? Before you make an interview appointment, research the job description and the company. Does the job provide the schedule and pay you require? What skills does the job require and do you have them? (If you can't lift more than twenty pounds, don't apply for UPS.) Is there a high turnover rate for the position? Would the job interfere with your personal values or priorities? Would you be your own boss or could you handle being a "yes-man?" Would you be willing to relocate, if necessary?

Second, consider the environment of the company. Some people prefer to work in more structured or traditional office environments, while others need a thriving, innovative atmosphere. What "mood" do you sense from the company? Would you feel stressed at the thought of having to walk through the doors every morning? Is the company known for too few or too many social gatherings? Is there a history of discrimination at the company that you don't want to deal with?

While you will probably be flattered by any job offer, you should like the job enough that you won't find yourself back at the tryout stage again in a few months, due to surprisingly horrible job conditions! So, know what to expect before you get hired.

Do They Want You?

A hiring company will determine the answer to this question by how professionally you present your cover letter and resume, application, and interview. Sometimes companies have a "love at first sight" feeling with a prospective employee, while other applicants encounter four or five interviews and meetings with executives before they sign you on. So, be prepared and be patient!

The first step of the application process is to submit a very polished cover letter and resume. Gear each resume you send toward the particular job for which you are applying, as well as to the type of company. Make sure your resume would grant you an 'A' in a technical writing class—no typos or glaring mistakes. Be original, but not too creative, unless you are applying for an artsy or advertising job.

In addition to your resume, you will have to fill out an application, which you will most likely write by hand. The employers will scrutinize this to see how legible your hand-writing is, so polish your third grade penmanship skills before you fill it out. Along with your application, you will prob-ably have to provide some sort of proof that you are a citizen (driver's license) and that you are not a criminal (Social Secu-rity card). Many jobs will require you to take a physical exam or drug test. If you want the job, comply—and make sure you can pass the tests.

And Finally, the Interview!

The two things that will matter most when the big guns put you under the lights are appearance and professionalism.

And no, for appearance, I am not saying you have to look like a supermodel to work at a consulting firm. But, you do have to look like a supermodel to be a supermodel. If you are interviewing for a corporate position, forget Friday's business casual look—instead, pay a visit to Brooks Brothers (and you will pay big bucks) and show up in a nice, professional business suit. Stick to simple colors and designs—solids are usually best. Wear something that flatters you and makes you feel comfortable. Girls, go easy on the makeup and jewelry, and try to look like someone the company would be proud to put in their brochure.

Professionalism

There's that word again. What does it mean? Turn off your nag filter and absorb this advice: Sit up straight, speak clearly and in complete sentences, don't chew gum, mind your manners, arrive fifteen minutes early, respect your elders, use a pleasant voice, and watch your grammar. Okay, now unplug your ears, but follow Mom's advice if you want to be taken seriously. Following are some sample interview questions that employers use all the time, accompanied with the questions they are really asking. Read them, study them, and formulate concise, scripted answers that you can deliver without sounding scripted.

- What are your greatest qualities? (*What are your strengths? Are you too quick to brag? Too slow to give yourself credit? How can we best use you?*)

- What are your greatest weaknesses? (*How glaring are these weaknesses? How quickly do you recall them? How can this weakness be turned into a strength? Where could this weakness be a problem?*)

- How well do you work in a team/with others? (*It doesn't matter if they lock you in a basement, they will still want you to be pleasant when they bring you your meals. You have to work well with others to be indispensable to a company.)*

- How do you handle stress? *(How do you calm yourself down? Solve problems? Avoid contention? Do you keep your cool? Do you thrive under pressure?)*

- Why do you want this job? *(Why are we wasting our time interviewing you?)*

- Why should we hire you over somebody else? *(Okay, give me your sales pitch—why are you better than the other guy waiting outside? How will you benefit us?)*

- What is your favorite color/animal/food/flower/season and how does it represent you? *(How do you see yourself? What can you come up with on the spot?)*

- What is your dream job? *(What are you passionate about? Are you ambitious? Am I going to have to worry about my job in a few years?)*

- Where do you see yourself in five years? *(How goal-oriented and ambitious are you?)*

- How do you handle conflict? *(Are you a problem solver or a problem maker?)*

- Tell me about the last place you worked. *(How well did you get along with the other people? Will you slander us when you leave here?)*

- Why did you leave your last job? *(Are you a complainer? What will you expect us to provide to keep you here, and can we provide it?)*

Remember to keep all of your answers concise, to the point, not overly wordy, directed toward the question, informative, brief, relevant, succinct, accurate, memorable, and precise. In other words, the exact opposite of what I just did—talk about annoying.

Making the Draft

On that glorious day, after many spent biting fingernails, toenails, and whatever else you can bite, you will receive a call or a letter with a job offer! While this will be a big relief (you're not a pathetic loser after all!), you have not yet made the team. First of all, if you are offered the job in person or over the phone, do not turn all drama queen on them and freak out like you won the lotto. If you appear too eager to have been offered a job, they know they will not have to negotiate your salary, or they will think you are a pathetic loser! Keep calm, but appear gracious. If you know without a doubt that the job is the right one for you, and you've considered all the factors (pay, hours, benefits, expectations, holidays, etc.), go ahead and politely accept by saying something like, "I look forward to working with you." If you are not sure if you want the job, ask for some time (preferably a day or two—not two months) to consider the offer.

You may want the job, but maybe you don't like the package that comes with it. Perhaps you were expecting a larger salary, more vacation time, or better benefits. If one of these factors really matters to you, by all means negotiate. Most companies are willing to appease you if they really want you. To do this, say something in the vein of, "As much as I would love this job, I really cannot work more than thirty-five hours a week because of my schooling/sick grandmother/ TV lineup"—but maybe don't use that last one. If you are polite while negotiating, and prove to the company that your request is fair and necessary, they will most likely meet you in the middle.

First String Line-Up

Making the team doesn't mean you will automatically play well and subsequently be re-signed the next season. To really build a successful career, you need to maintain certain job skills that will deem you an asset and not a liability to the company. Pay heed to these do's and don'ts (taken from real people's work experiences), and you will be a candidate for "Employee of the Month," which may give you a better parking space!

Do: Be ethical. Just because something may not be against company policy does not mean it is the right thing to do.
Don't: Justify everything as being owed to you. No, the company does not owe you a few pens for your home office just because you worked late last night.

Do: Be responsible.
Don't: Leave a sign on an open register that says, "Be back in fifteen minutes," or take a nap on the floor when business is slow.

Do: Be honest.
Don't: Fudge on your time cards and business expenses, comingle funds, and assume credit you don't deserve.

Do: Be respectful (to your superiors and customers, as well as the janitors and receptionists).
Don't: Yell at your boss just because she is "a chick" and younger than you are (That jerk!).

Do: Be on time—or even better, early! And always call if you can't be.
Don't: Just never show up—ever, ever again.

Do: Be a team player. If you are, you'll get a cake and a party thrown in your honor when you move on to bigger and better things.
Don't: Be the person who everyone tries to get fired because you are lazy, stupid, smelly, and/or mean.

Do: Be classy.

Don't: Discuss personal matters (your sex life, your salary, what you did to get hired) with your coworkers.

Do: Be ambitious. Every day, do three extra things to improve your work.
Don't: Just punch in, blindly follow your to-do list, and leave five minutes early, unless you never, ever want a raise or promotion.

Do: Learn names. (Mentally repeat them three times, or draw them on your hand with your finger.)
Don't: Call a person by the wrong name for an entire year.

Do: Flatter your boss.
Don't: Blame your boss for everything.

Do: Have a life outside work.
Don't: Earn a tombstone with the words: "He sure worked hard."

Do: Read self-improvement books and continue your skills training and education.
Don't: Let that brain dissolve into mush by never trying to grow, improve, or learn.

Quitting Time

So, it finally happened—they benched you for the third straight game! Or, you got a better offer from another team. One day, you may decide you've learned all you can, the salary just ain't enough, you are moving nowhere on your personal career ladder, your house plants need more attention, or you just can't stand your boss's leering glances when you wear knee-length skirts. Quitting is okay if you do it for the right reasons, as long as you are professional and tactful.

To be fair, when you quit, most companies appreciate at least a "two-week notice," meaning you are giving them two weeks to replace you. Others may be happy to get rid of your benched butt! When you quit, offer to help train your replacement, and leave all of your work in legible form. You should provide some sort of reason why you are quitting, and once you do leave, do not slander the company.

You must be tactful if you plan on getting a decent reference out of the company in the future. When you resign, don't tell them you are "so glad to finally be free!" or that you just "hate it here soooo much!" While you should provide some sort of a reason for your departure, do not get too graphic. They would rather hear that you have "family problems" than that you have a delusional uncle that stalks you and your peers, and you must get away (unless you work at *The National Enquirer*). It may be best to resign by a letter or during a set appointment with your boss. Explain your position professionally, and you will avoid burning a bridge you may later need.

Fired!

Oh you dirty little rat! You said you were taking off this week to attend your "grandmother's funeral," but after you returned to work, your grandmother really took a spill that required a funeral! Or, when your boss at the feed store asked you what you thought of his new "hoe," you assumed he was talking about his new girlfriend . . .

Well, it's okay, many people get fired and survive. If you do get fired, try to learn from the experience so you won't repeat the mistake at your next job. If possible, try to salvage what you can and clarify the heinous thing you did that got you canned. Then, maybe you have a chance at some sort of redeeming referral; although, I wouldn't recommend listing bosses who fired you as a future reference for another job! Gather up your desktop supplies, your last paycheck, and move on! Time for a different sport.

chapter 14

From the Bank to the Balance Book: How to Set Up, Balance, and Build Your Account

How fat is your nest egg?

1. A bounced check _____.
   a. Is made out of rubber
   b. Is sooo embarrassing!
   c. Is a sign of financial irresponsibility

2. Saving money _____.
   a. Hinders my wardrobe growth
   b. Is something I'll start doing in a few years
   c. Is vital to ensure a secure future

3. "ATM" stands for _____.
   a. At the mall
   b. All that money!
   c. Automated teller machine

If you scored:

Mostly a's: Your birds are starving.
Mostly b's: Your nest has holes.
Mostly c's: Your nest is harvesting in a nice palm tree in Barbados!

Do you marvel at the machines from which money magically appears? Do you write checks until your checkbook is empty, even if your account was barren long ago? Do you think "investing" is a hobby of the old and rich—something that will never apply to you? Do you really believe money grows on trees? If your parents pampered you with an "emergency credit card" to Banana Republic and a hefty allowance, you may be a little naïve in the financial world. There are many who have suffered from the aforementioned financial diseases; not only are their birds starving, they don't even know what a "nest egg" is.

Financial debts and obligations are perhaps the most stressful encounters you will have with adult life. Money problems regularly factor in emotional stress, crime, and divorce. But if you learn while you are young how to take care of today and prepare for tomorrow financially, you will be a much more happy, successful person. This chapter will take you through financial basics like how to choose a bank, set up and balance your accounts, and start investing now so you can retire before you are once again bald and wearing diapers.

Choosing Your Dough's Safe House

A bank or a credit union? The mom-and-pop place down the street, or a large, nationwide institution? The place with free checking, or the place with free checks? There are actually a lot of factors to consider when you are ready to open an account, the most important being that you choose a financial institution that is FDIC insured. (That means that in case of a bank failure, the government will insure your money up to $250,000.) If you are a student, you may want to join a bank that provides a specialized student account, because it will be more tailored to a first-time banking client. Consider the following options as well.

Banks Versus Credit Unions

There are pros and cons to each. A bank conveniently provides many services to assist you in your money management. Banks are usually part of a chain, so ATM locations are more accessible, which makes traveling to other states easier if you get in a bind. On the other hand, banks are businesses. That is—they are more profit-oriented than service-oriented, charging more fees and penalties than a credit union will.

Credit unions are non-profit organizations that provide the same services that a bank does. The downsides? To join, you must be affiliated with the credit union's sponsor, which is usually a neighborhood, place of employment, school, or other private organization. And, credit unions are not part of a national chain, so you will be charged more ATM fees if you are not near your credit union's headquarters. Even if you do not do all of your primary banking with a credit union, it is a great place to take out a loan, as your fees and interest rates may be lower.

How Convenient!

How close is your bank to your house or work? Does your bank have chains across the nation? If you are out of town, will there be a teller or ATM that can save you if you did not bring enough cash or traveler's checks? What are the hours your bank is open? Do they offer telephone banking services? Online banking? Do they have conveniently located twenty-four-hour ATMs that do not charge phenomenal fees? Consider all of these issues of convenience when picking your bank.

Hey! What's That For?

You may be as happy as a clam when you finally set up your account, but your first banking statement may feature a whole list of hidden costs and mysterious charges. Thus, when you first go to the bank, ask for all of the fine print regulations on the following services. (Also, read any mail you may receive from the bank to check for subsequent policy changes.)

Monthly Service Fees

Fees, usually no more than $5 each, may be deducted from your accounts every month as "ATM fees," "checking fees" or "account fees." See if these can be waived if you maintain a minimum balance in your account, open up more than one account, or apply for a student account. Also, steer clear of any institution that charges you each time you write a check or use your ATM card. A very rich man owns those banks!

Overdraft Protection

Okay, say you are not perfect at balancing your checkbook, and one month you accidentally write a check for more than you have in your account. Most banks and credit unions offer overdraft protection—usually for a fee—that prevents you from bouncing checks up to a limit, by supplementing the amount you go over. They will either deduct it from your savings account, or just charge you for the overdraft on your next statement. While you should not be a habitual overdrafter, it is better to have this service than to be charged.

Check Bouncing Penalties

"NSF" stands for "non-sufficient funds," and it is not an abbreviation you want to see on a letter addressed to you. If you do not have overdraft protection and you write a check for more than your account can cover, you have "non-sufficient funds" and will be penalized. The bank will kick you in the rear with a fine of up to $35, and the place you wrote your check to will charge you a similar fine from the other end. Check your bank's NSF penalties, or better yet, don't bounce checks!

Minimum Balances

Many banks will require you to maintain a minimum balance in your checking, savings, or money market account for it to be worthwhile for them to keep you as a customer. (They are earning interest from the money you invest.) Try to avoid minimum balance regulations in accounts you use often, and watch out for fees if you dip below the minimum required balance.

Fraud Protection

So, what happens if someone swipes your purse or wallet? Besides having to stand in long lines at the DMV, Social Security office, and student ID center, you are going to have to get new account numbers if your credit cards, ATM cards, and checkbooks disappear. Your bank should not hold you liable for fraudulent charges of more than $50 and should set up your new accounts for little to no fee. Check beforehand to make sure you are protected against fraud, and report any lost or stolen wallets immediately!

Which Banking Services to Establish

So, which accounts should you open? Which cards should you leave your new bank or credit union with? Following are the standard services you can request.

Checking/ATM Account

These are the most essential banking privileges. Basically, you have an account that you deposit money into, either by filling out the requested information on a deposit slip (found in the back of your checkbook), or by making a "direct deposit," in which you establish a system whereby a weekly or monthly expected earning (such as a paycheck or money from pops) is automatically submitted into your account. The money is then available for your use as a withdrawal or payment. If you want to write a check, it's really quite self-explanatory. Just write the desired information in the provided area.

It usually takes a couple of days to process a check after it is written, so you will have a little time to make sure the money to cover the check is in your account. If you don't want to write a check but want to use the money in your checking account, you can get a check card, also known as an ATM card. An ATM card deducts money directly from your account when you use it, so make sure the money is in your account, or you will be susceptible to non-sufficient funds fines. An ATM card is used much like a credit card, except you also have to enter a PIN (Personal Identification Number) to ensure that you are the rightful user. The major perks to this kind of card are that you can get additional cash back at the same time you make your purchase at a grocery store and you can access twenty-four-hour, convenient ATMs if you need moolah at midnight.

Savings Account

Whether you are saving short-term for a new bike, or long-term for a new car, it is safe to put your money in an FDIC-approved savings account. Because of inflation, the money you deposit into your savings account earns interest. So, the longer your money remains in the account, the more interest it earns. Savings accounts have low interest rates so you will not earn as much as you would investing it in stocks or bonds, but generally, a savings account is less risky. And if an emergency arises, you should not have any problems withdrawing your money from a savings account or transferring it to your checking account.

Money Market Account

A money market account is a savings account with a higher interest rate. But it is a more risky investment, because money markets are not FDIC insured. You can still easily access the money from your market account if you need to.

Bank-Issued Credit Card

Your bank may also issue you a credit card. This account will be treated as a normal, separate account from your checking and savings. To understand credit cards more fully, read Chapter Fifteen.

Traveler's Check

When Spring Break rolls around, you do not want to be a thief's target carrying around a fat wad of cash in case the foreign lands and swapmeet vendors do not take credit cards. Go to your bank and get traveler's checks, which are checks issued with preset amounts and designed to be more secure than regular checks, because you have to present ID and sign the check in the presence of the recipient.

Cashier's Check

Again, when you don't want to risk carrying a briefcase full of cash, but you need to pay somebody a large sum of money that is immediately good for his or her use, have your bank or your local 7-Eleven issue you a cashier's check. For a small fee, they will verify that you have the money to cover the check, then they will issue a bank-certified check that can be immediately cashed by the recipient.

Loan

So, you finally saved up the money to buy your car! But, you can only afford half of it. That doesn't mean you don't get the car; it means you need a loan. Banks and credit unions are popular places to take out loans, especially if you are a long-standing, responsible member of the branch. To apply for a loan, you basically need to convince the lender that he can trust you, based on your job stability and a good financial history. The lender will give the other half of the money to the car dealer, if you contractually promise to pay the lender back over a specified time. It's not as peachy as it sounds, because you will also be paying an interest rate on the amount you borrowed. The loan is a debt and should not be treated lightly. While it got you your wheels, it can also screw up your credit and repossess your car, if you don't make your loan payments.

Bank Statement

Your bank should provide you with a monthly statement, either by mail or online, that lists all of your deposits, withdrawals, cleared checks, card uses, loan information, fees and fines. Always check your statement and compare it to your records to make sure they are accurate. "Bank errors" are common, and not just when you are playing Monopoly. Except in real life, the bank usually doesn't pay you $200 for their mistakes.

What Do I Do Now?

Once you have established all of your accounts, there is work to do to maintain them if you don't want your bank to charge you fines up the wazoo. You need to be responsible with your earning, spending, and saving. The only way to do this is to *keep a record* of all of your transactions! Sure, the bank will send you a statement every month listing your available balance, and sure, you can punch a few buttons on your computer to see how much money you have left, but you are not going to want to carry your bank statements or your computer to Fatburger with you, to see if you can afford a shake! You need to keep an ongoing tally of how much you earn and where it is spent. Of the following, pick the method that works for you and stick to it!

Quicken and Receipts

If you are computer-savvy, invest in Microsoft's most recent Quicken program, and learn it. Throughout the day, as you buy books, concert tickets, and Powerade, keep all of your receipts in a safe place in your wallet or purse. Then, every night, enter your expenses into Quicken, and see how much money you have left for the next day, week, or month. The great thing about Quicken is that it will show you month-to-date and year-to-date updates, including pie charts that itemize where you are going over budget. Also, it makes tax time very easy, as you have printable proof as to where your money has evaporated throughout the year.

Ledger

Most checkbooks and some credit and ATM cards come with a ledger book in which you can keep track of all of your transactions. The most important factor in using ledgers successfully is to make sure you maintain one updated master ledger for all of the different methods of spending and users of the same account. To maintain your ledger, always keep a running balance of the money you have available. Then, for each transaction, submit the date, amount, and source of spending or receiving funds. Add or subtract the amount from the balance, like this:

Date	Transaction	Amount +/-	Balance
			+$232.14
3/12	Groceries— Greg's Groceries	– $44.70	+$187.44
3/14	Paycheck— Papa Joe's	+ $530. 00	+$717.44
3/14	Gas—Arco	– $22.09	+$695.35

The Memory Method

Most often used by housewives and despised by working husbands, this method is the simplest and most faulty of them all. When you make a purchase, simply "remember it"—the amount, the date, where you spent it. Subtract that amount from how much you think you have in your account, and keep a running total. Try not to suffer amnesia, because then you are in for it. I really do not recommend this method (and neither does my husband).

Put Some Away For Later

Investing is not something you should wait to begin "in a few years"—a perpetual phrase. The earlier you start saving, the bigger your retirement yacht will be! In fact, if you start putting $2,000 a year in a Roth IRA account at a 10 percent interest rate when you are fifteen, by the time you are sixty-five, you will have $2.3 million. But, keep in mind inflation will cut the spending value in half, so you may want to invest a few other ways, as well.

While FDIC-insured banks are very safe havens for all of your hard-earned income, you may want to use higher interest rates to make your money grow even faster. There are several ways to do this—most are risky, but if you play the game right, most are profitable, as well. The two rules of investing are (1) to understand what you are doing and (2) to diversify your investments. If you are not equipped with a decent level of investment know-how, meet with an investment agent who will usually start your portfolio at little to no charge. And if you do not diversify your investments, you may end up like an Enron employee, cheated out of a lifetime of investments because of a company's false promises and failure! Following are the most basic ways you can invest your money. (If you really want to understand how investments work, read *Rich Dad, Poor Dad* by Robert Kiyosaki, TechPress, Inc.).

Stock Market

In decent economic times, a little money can go a long way in the stock market. If you're thinking about playing the market, you will need to open an investment account. Buying stock is buying ownership shares in a company. If the company does well, then the value of the stock rises, creating a profit. If you then sell your shares of stock, you will make an increase in the money you invested. If you keep your money invested in a company for a long time, the company could split, merge with another, or get bought out, and your shares may raise significantly in value! The stock market is risky, though, because at any time, a company you're interested in could go bankrupt, the economy could do poorly, or the market could crash, and you could be out a lot of money! To play it safe, really research the stocks in which you invest and, most importantly, diversify! If all your eggs are in one basket, you're done for if your basket files for bankruptcy.

Bond Market

If you take out a bond, you are loaning a sum of your money to another person, who guarantees to repay you the money over a specific amount of time, plus interest. Like your savings account, bonds are a safer investment than stocks but do not have the growth potential and high rate of return that stocks can bring. But, what you trade in growth opportunities is made up for in security.

CD's (Certificates of Deposits)

CD's are similar to bonds, in that you are committing to keeping a sum of money locked into an account for a specific amount of time. You will earn high interest rates on CD's, but again, you cannot touch the money for a designated amount of time, without paying a fee.

Mutual Funds

Mutual funds are professionally managed funds. You entrust a sum of money to a financial institution that will then diversify your money into stocks and bonds that fall under a category, like technology or health care. Mutual funds provide a great way for new investors to become familiar with the market, while allowing a seasoned professional to do the work.

IRA's

You can contribute up to $3,000 tax-free annually to an IRA (Individual Retirement Account) fund. The money is tax-deferred, meaning you do not pay taxes on it until you withdraw it; and the money you invest is not counted as taxable income for the year in which you invest it.

Roth IRA's

Roth IRA's follow the same rules as the traditional IRA's; but instead of paying the taxes on your investment later, you pay them when you invest in your account. The great thing about Roth IRA's is when you cash yours in several years from now, you do not have to pay any taxes on the increased amount (because you already have).

401k's

Through your place of employment, you may be able to deduct a specified amount of your paycheck and contribute it each month to your 401k plan. The money is deducted first from your yearly earnings and taxable income, placing you in a lower tax bracket, although you will have to pay the taxes on the fund when you withdraw it.

Altogether, investing is a game, with really high stakes—your financial well-being! But, if you know what you are doing and are blessed with skill and luck, you will enjoy your profits! You can keep track of your investments online or in the financial section of daily newspapers. Just be leery of "hot tips," new, mysterious companies, and typing errors in picking your stocks, if you invest online.

When you are on your own, you will hopefully learn the importance of managing your financial affairs with as much interest as you mind your Twitter following. Forming good financial habits now will pave a golden road to your future in Barbados!

chapter 15

The Seven-Year Mistake: Understanding Credit

What kind of card are you pre-approved for?

1. Who would most likely say this about you: "Give her some credit."
    a. Your mom
    b. Your boss
    c. The credit bureau

2. "APR" stands for _____.
    a. All-night Party at Rob's!
    b. April?
    c. Annual Percentage Rate

3. The "bureau" you most fear is _____.
    a. The credit bureau
    b. The Better Business Bureau
    c. The FBI

If you scored:

Mostly a's: $50 limit!
Mostly b's: $500 limit!
Mostly c's: $50,000 limit!

As soon as you turn eighteen, your mailbox becomes host to a variety of offers promoting magic cards that buy things, without you having to pay for them right away! Yup—these cards will get you groceries, new clothes, CD's, even cars! Your first credit card will really christen you to the mantle of adulthood in the Real World, but it is very important to understand how they work. Credit cards are very dangerous, and they can have long term effects on your financial life if you do not understand how they work.

FAQ's

Following are some of the most frequently asked questions about credit cards. Knowing the answers can save you a lot of money and stress!

How Does Credit Work?

Credit cards can be your convenient shopping friend or your worst enemy—if you abuse them. The company that grants you a credit card is basically loaning you money to make purchases, and by signing the contract agreement, you are promising to pay the lender back within a certain amount of time, or interest is incurred. When it comes to credit cards, interest is the key word!

With your credit card, you can make purchases from vendors who accept your card type, but you can't exceed the credit limit you were given. Your first credit card will have a low limit, like $500. After you make a purchase, you will have a grace period of about twenty-five days to pay your balance to the credit card company. In that amount of time, you will receive a bill that states how much you owe and when it's due. You can pay your bill by mailing in a check; or with most cards, you can submit a payment online, by phone, or by setting up an automatic withdrawal from your bank account. While credit cards are a really simple way to pay for purchases, they are risky if you do not pay off your balance right away. The longer you wait to pay your bill, the more money you will have to pay.

While recent high school graduates receive credit card offers from all over the planet, remember there is a reason they are enticing *you* with cards in all varieties of metal. Credit card companies know that financial amateurs may be very eager to make purchases they can not afford, just because they can. And they know that you probably do not yet know the impacts of interest and debt. You see, everything that you charge to a credit card, because there is not enough money in your budget to pay for it, requires twice the amount of work to pay it back. If you make $1,000 a month, and buy a $500 stereo that you really can't afford, not only will you have to come up with the $500 plus interest to pay for the stereo, but you will have to earn an extra $500 to cover the costs of what you sacrificed paying for to cover the stereo bill. Because it may take you a while to do this, you are in debt longer and thus owe more interest to the credit card company.

Credit card debt is a perpetual cycle that you don't want to enter. Learn now how to use credit cards wisely to build your credit and not hurt it.

What Is Interest? How Does It Work?

Over time, the worth of a dollar lessens with the economy's inflation. So, if you borrow $100 from a friend, and then pay him back one year later, you are actually shortchanging him because the $100 will not be worth as much as it used to be. Interest rates were developed to allow lenders to loan people money, with the knowledge that they would be paid back plus some—with the incentive of interest. Since most credit card companies charge interest rates on your purchases that are much higher than the increased value of money due to inflation, credit card issuers make money—and lots of it!

Credit cards are accompanied with an "APR"—or annual percentage rate. Here is an easy way to understand the concept of APR. If you buy shoes that cost $100 and carry a debt of $100 over a year, your credit card company will charge you a certain percent of that $100 as interest for not paying the money back within the year. If your APR is 12 percent (a typical credit card rate), and if you maintain a $100 balance over a year, you will have to pay the company $112 to fully pay your debt. If inflation of the economy is only 2 percent, then the credit card company is profiting $10 from your debt. That is why they are so eager to give you a card.

Let's say you pay the $100 back in three months. You will still be charged an interest rate starting the day your grace period ends, but it will be much less than if you waited a year. To figure out your monthly percentage rate, divide the number of months in a year (twelve) by your APR. That is how much interest you will pay each month. Many companies even calculate interest to the day; to figure this out, divide 365 by your APR.

But What If I Get a Card Offering a Zero Percent APR, or a Low Introductory APR?

These offers are common when a company is trying to get your name added to their list of clientele. They entice you with a low-interest or interest-free period to get you to sign up, but then they bump you up to a regular interest rate a short amount of time later. Credit cards with low interest rates are great if you can pay off your purchase before the regular interest rate sets in; but if you wait until the introductory rate time period is over to pay your balance, you will have to back pay a high interest rate on all of your outstanding debt (and that rate is usually really high). If you have a credit card that is carrying a high balance, it may be prudent for you to transfer that balance to a card with a lower interest rate; but try to avoid doing this too much because opening a lot of new accounts greatly affects your credit rating.

So Why Should I Mess Around with Credit Cards?

Why should you even get a credit card if they are so bad? Ask all those people who have never had one why they can't get approved to buy a house, unless they have all the cash upfront to pay for it. Sometime in your life, you will encounter a large, necessary debt, like a car or a house. In order for you to get a loan for these necessities, you must have a good credit rating. And the only way to get a good credit rating is to show that you have had credit cards and debts that you have paid off on time! So, it is good to go ahead and get at least one widely accepted card (Visa, Mastercard, Discover, and American Express are the most universal), and use it wisely. If you want to shop around for different cards to see which one is best for you, check out the website: *www. creditcardrates.com.*

I Can't Get a Card Because I Have No Credit History! This Doesn't Make Sense!

If you have never had a credit card before, you will have no credit history, which may make it difficult for a credit company to trust you enough to issue you a card. Try to get a card issued from your bank, or one that is geared toward students and first-time credit applicants, like Citibank. They will start you out with a lower limit and a higher interest rate, but this is a good opportunity for you to prove to yourself and future lenders that you are responsible enough to have a credit card. All of your credit history is available to lenders on your credit report.

What Is My Credit Report?

Say there are two high school students running for student body president. Kid Number One has a 4.0 GPA, no absences or tardies, and has always been involved with student government. Kid Number Two maintains a C average, misses school often, and never participates in any school activities. Who should you vote for? Obvious, right—unless Kid Two is your best friend. Well, that's how your credit report works. Whenever you want to borrow money from a lender, apply for a credit card, or prove to a service-related company that you will be reliable with your payments, the lender or company will check your credit report.

Your credit report is like a report card. It will have all of your vital information—your name, current and previous addresses, Social Security number, date of birth, employer's names and your marital status. It also contains a specific record of all of your financial history—how long you have had credit, how many different cards you have had, the various loans and debts you have, whether you pay them on time, and how many times you have tried to open new credit lines. If applicable, your credit report will also list any bankruptcies, tax liens, and court judgments regarding your financial history. And, it will have your credit score or rating.

What is My Credit Score?

On your credit report, you will have a score ranging from 375 to 900. Scores above 600 are considered good, but your number's significance changes with a particular lender's guidelines. People who have proven responsible with their credit history will have higher scores and a better chance of qualifying for a loan or credit line. Your credit score improves for every good, responsible thing you do financially. The best way to improve your score is to consistently pay your bills on time. It is okay to carry a balance on your credit card as long as you can pay it off in a minimal amount of time. In fact, paying off a debt gradually actually boosts your score, as long as you make the minimum payments each month. But, try not to use more than 75 percent of your available credit limit, because maxing out your credit cards does not help. Other ways to improve your credit score are to close all of your credit accounts that you don't use and to avoid applying for too many different credit cards.

How Can I Get a Copy of My Credit Report?

There are three credit agencies that are widely used by lenders when considering a credit or loan applicant. For a fee (around $30), they will send you your personalized credit report. Here is their contact information:

Experian   P.O. Box 2106
        Allen, TX 75013-2106
        1-800-422-4879
        www.experian.com

TransUnion   P.O. Box 390
        Springfield, PA 19064
        1-800-916-8800
        www.transunion.com

Equifax   P.O. Box 740241
        Atlanta, GA 30374-0241
        1-800-685-1111
        www.equifax.com

Although these credit bureaus provide your credit information to requesting lenders, they do not make the actual lending decision when you apply for an account or a loan. They merely provide your information (your FICO score) to the lender. If you are denied credit when you apply for it, you have the right to know why. The creditor may immediately tell you why, or you have the right to request the reason within sixty days. If you were denied credit because of information on your credit report, you can contact the bureau, and you are entitled to receive a copy of your report.

How Often Does My Credit Rating Change?

Your credit rating changes every time you make a purchase, pay a bill, or pay a debt—essentially every day. Your positive credit experiences stay on your record indefinitely, but other information like unused or closed accounts, public record information, and negative information like bankruptcies can stay on your credit report for at least seven years. Credit inquiries usually stay on your report for up to two years.

How Can I Dispute Something on My Credit Report That Is Not Correct?

The law allows you to dispute incorrect information on your credit report, without cost. If you see an error, just call or write to the credit bureau, and they will send you a response within thirty days. If you disagree with their response, you can add a statement of contest to your report, for future lenders to see.

My Credit Card Offers a Cash Advance Service. What Is This?

Some credit cards allow you to take out cash from an ATM—up to a certain limit (which is much lower than your regular credit limit). Beware, however, because interest on cash advances is usually much higher than credit purchases and is usually immediately retroactive.

What Fees Do Credit Cards Charge?

Some credit card companies charge annual fees for their services, but they are usually no more than $50. While it is better to have a card with no fees, some of the cards that do offer fees make up for it with lower APR's and other perks. You may also acquire penalty fees from your card issuer for late payments and for exceeding your credit limit. These fees are in the ballpark of $25, but your company may waive your first penalty as a warning.

My Card Offers a "Cash-Back" Program. What Is This?

Some cards offer perks by granting you points for every dollar you spend. These points can be cashed in for items such as airline tickets, hotel and travel vouchers, dining and shopping certificates, and other rewards. Check the specifics with your card issuer.

What Do I Do If My Card Is Lost or Stolen?

First of all, as soon as you receive a card in the mail, you should sign the space provided in the back. Then photocopy the front and back of your card so you have record of your account number, the type of card, and the card issuer's contact information that is listed on the back of the card. Keep this record in a safe place. There should be a phone number issued specifically for lost or stolen cards. If your card is then lost or stolen, call that number immediately and report it. The issuer should not hold you liable for any fraudulent charges more than $50 and should reissue you a new card and account number.

What If There Are Charges on My Account Statement That I Did Not Make?

Call your credit card company and verify the charges. You may just have forgotten that you actually did spend $250 at Costco (happens to me). If the charges were not made by you, report it to the company as fraud and contest paying it. They can research the charge and remove it from your statement.

What If I Just Really Screw Up and Get into Major Debt That I Just Can't Pay?

If you have several cards with outstanding balances, try to prioritize which one to pay down first by which card has the highest interest rate. As you pay off each card, cut it up or hide it, and try to make all your future purchases with cash until you are out of debt.

If you really get in over your head, see a debt counselor, or contact the National Foundation for Credit Counseling (1-800-388-2227/*www.nfcc.org*) for free or low-cost counseling. They can help you consolidate your debts into one affordable payment each month with a manageable interest rate. You may have to work a few extra hours and cut down on your budget to get your debts paid off, but it is worth it to eliminate the financial stress and harassing phone calls of collections agencies.

If you have just really come to financial duress, your debt counselor may recommend you file for bankruptcy, as a last resort. If you file for bankruptcy, you are not legally held to all of your debts, though you may be asked to pay them over time. But don't misunderstand bankruptcy as an easy solution to debt. Bankruptcy stays on your credit report for seven to ten years, and its very presence on your report will discourage landlords from renting to you, employers from hiring you, lenders from loaning you any money—and you will probably not be trusted with a credit card (which may not be a bad idea).

As you see, credit cards can be a blessing or a burden, depending on how you use them. Remember, you're in the Real World now, so use them wisely!

chapter 16

Pay Now . . . Or Pay Later:
Understanding Insurance

Could you sell insurance?

1. A deductible is _____.
   a. A table made out of duct tape
   b. A stipulated amount an insured person has to pay before an insurance company will cover a cost

2. A premium is _____.
   a. A type of steak
   b. A periodic amount you pay to maintain your insurance coverage

3. A policy is _____.
   a. A female police officer
   b. A contract in which one party guarantees to insure another party against a loss, if that person pays a premium

---

If you scored:

Mostly a's: Nope
Mostly b's: Yup

Okay all you daredevils who love street racing, catfights, and bungee jumping, I'd like you to meet . . . insurance. While the young and free never think anything bad will happen to them, you need to plan now for the unexpected. Granted, paying insurance premiums is so annoying because obviously someone like *you* will never wreck your car, break your leg, or, um—die (knock on wood). But there are people who do these things every single day, and because of them, the rest of us have to pay. Insurance follows a simple concept—you pay a little now, and some large corporation foots the big bills later if something unexpected ever does happen to you. Or, you can just press your luck hoping you remain in your perfect form for time and all eternity, and then file bankruptcy when you do get rear-ended by an uninsured motorist. It's always better to have insurance; in fact, some types of insurance are required by law. So, when you are kicked out of your house and into the Real World, make sure someone is paying your premiums!

Insurance! I Don't Need No Stinkin' Insurance! (Do I?)

If you knew that "b" was the correct answer for all three quiz answers, you probably understand how insurance works. But, for all of you who skipped out on any conversation your parents ever had regarding "all those !@#$ bills," here is an example of how and why you need it.

Let's say you get a new car that is so absolutely beautiful, you would enter into a deep depression if someone ever dented it. Though you would prefer never to have an accident rather than have to get your car pounded and painted back to its perfect form if someone did hit you, you want to take all the safety precautions. So, you take out an insurance policy with State Farm. Your policy states that if you pay a bi-annual premium (a bill) of $800, they will cover any damages or losses to your car during that time. One day, some idiot talking on her cell phone hits you, and you need a new fender and paint job. Price tag: $2,400. You can't afford that! But, lucky for you—you don't have to. Her insurance company covers the bill and rents you a car while you wait for the repairs. What if she is not insured? Besides the fact that she will probably be fined, ticketed, and have her license taken away, your insurance policy should have an "uninsured motorist" clause (make sure it does!), so your company will foot the bill. If not, consider yourself unlucky, and get a second job—or walk from now on.

What if the accident was your fault? If you have insurance, your company will pay all damages both to your car and hers; and if anyone was injured, it should pick up the hospital bills as well. But, you will have to pay a deductible upwards of $250, and your next insurance policy premium will probably be higher. If you get in several wrecks that are all your fault in a short period of time, you may lose your insurance because it will either become astronomically unaffordable, or the company may drop you because you are too big of a liability.

And what if you pay $800 every six months for the rest of your life, and never have to make a claim because you live in a town of absolutely perfect drivers? Yup, you're out all of your money, your insurance company loves you for funding the food at their office parties, but—better safe than sorry.

Types of Insurance

There are several types of insurance you will need in your life. They all operate similar to the previous example of auto insurance. There are also several insurance companies that offer each type of insurance. Just like if you were buying a new bike or car, you should shop around when it comes to insurance rates. The quality of your policies and amount of your premiums will vary substantially from company to company. Obviously, you want to keep your quality high (watch out for company names you have not heard of) and your premiums low.

To compare rates, log on to one of several websites like *www.theinsuranceworks.com,* which offers free quotes. Or just flip through the millions of pages in the phonebook that are solely devoted to insurance companies.

Keep in mind that some insurance companies offer services for just one type of insurance, like auto, while others infiltrate several different types. The more policies you purchase through one company, the lower your premiums for each separate policy will be. Also, the longer you stay with a particular insurance company without having filed a significant number of claims, the better your chances of keeping your premiums low. Don't forget to update your insurer with your current address and to renew your policy whenever it expires—your renewal statement may not reach you if you forget to change your address. It sure wouldn't be pretty if you paid $200 a month for six years for health insurance, then had to pay a $3,500 bill because you forgot to renew your policy before you fell off your roof!

While many celebrities allegedly have insurance policies for their various famous body parts, the average person will not need too many policies, especially as a recent high school graduate. You will definitely want auto and health insurance. You may want to consider dental and renter's/homeowner's insurance. In a few years, you might look into life, disability, and long-term care insurance policies. And whenever you own anything that is worth a substantial amount of money and may appeal to a thief, go ahead and insure it! Here are some facts to consider when shopping for each policy.

Auto Insurance

This is a type of insurance that the law requires all drivers to carry. Each state has specific regulations for how extensively a driver must be insured, so check out the specifics with your local DMV. When you apply for auto insurance, the company will request copies of your license and driving record, which will list any accidents or citations you have had. A good auto insurance policy should pay a reasonable amount of restitution in case any of the following should happen:

- Comprehensive (do you park in dark alleys?)
- Collision (you get in an accident, whether it's your fault or you are hit by an uninsured motorist)
- Bodily injury (did the ambulance have to come?)
- Uninsured motorist bodily injury (dang that driver!)
- Medical expenses (those Band-Aids ain't free!)
- You may also want to consider adding the following perks to your policy:
- Towing (stranded at the drive-in?)
- Windshield replacement (don't drive behind big trucks on gravel roads)
- Auto rental (if your car's being fixed, and your bike has a flat . . .)

Most auto insurers offer discounts to their drivers, if they qualify. Some of the most common discounts are the following:

- Good Driver (no major accidents or tickets in a specified time)
- Occupational (are you a teacher? engineer?)

- Good student? (see if your insurance company gives a whoop)

- How much you drive (how many miles to and from work, etc.)

- Are you a "mature driver?" (hopefully not if you are reading this book)

- Driver's Education Graduate (did you watch the crash test videos?)

- Vehicle Security (does your car have an alarm? lo-jack? tracking device? do you park in a covered space? a garage? live in a gated community?)

- Group/Fleet Discount (is there more than one driver on your policy?)

Check with your auto insurance company regularly to see if you are qualified for any additional discount options they may have added. Once you have a policy, you will be issued at least two insurance cards—one for your car, and one for your wallet. Always keep them in those two spots in case you get into an accident!

Health Insurance

Even if you are in good health, you never know when you may spring a mysterious case of shingles or mono (which both love to attack innocent college students). And you don't want to learn the hard way that staying in a hospital for as little as one night costs over $1,000! Make sure you have health insurance, and carry your card with you wherever you go!

If you are single and under twenty-five, most states allow you to be covered by your parents' policy. But if that is not an option, check the available policies issued by your employer, commonly referred to in the hiring process as your "benefits package." If you qualify with your employer's group policy, you will receive medical benefits, and a discounted premium will most likely be taken out of your paycheck or be billed to you. If you don't have that option, your school may offer a student policy, often for a discounted rate if you use campus medical facilities. You may also qualify for benefits through a private or minority group. If none of these options work, you can apply through an independent company, but your premiums will be high. Or, if you fit the income or disability profiles, government programs such as Medicare and Medicaid may cover you.

Health insurance premiums usually do not increase based on how sick or accident prone you are, but many companies have the right to deny you coverage if you have extensive pre-existing medical conditions. Thus, before you get approved for a policy, you may have to complete a physical exam. Whether or not you smoke, drink, eat healthfully, and exercise may lower your premiums—and your risk for health problems!

When you take out a health policy, you are covered up to a certain limit for preventive, diagnostic, and treatment procedures. Some policies provide full coverage, while others offer 80/20 (you pay 20 percent), 90/10, or require you to pay out-of-pocket expenses or office co-pays. When you choose a policy, make sure it is tailored to your needs and the procedures you would most likely require. Recent television specials and movies have dramatized patients going postal on hospitals and insurance providers. While this is extreme behavior, there is some truth to the desperation parents and patients feel when they can not afford a life-saving or otherwise necessary medical treatment that is not covered by their policy.

When you choose an insurance company, you might be able to choose your specific type of policy. Besides government subsidized programs like Medicaid and Medicare, PPO's and HMO's are the two most popular options for healthcare. Policies that allow you to pick your own doctors and treatment facilities within a network (PPO's, or Preferred Provider Organizations) are more flexible about treatments and specialists but are usually more expensive. HMO's (Health Maintenance Organizations) are more affordable but are more stringent about which treatments, doctors, and facilities are approved within your network. Whatever you choose, just always make sure you have good health insurance, because you never know what could happen!

Dental Insurance

Most people don't visit a dentist more than once a year—to their dentists' displeasure. So, most people do not have dental insurance, because they figure whatever they would spend on a premium is more than what they spend on their checkups. But anyone who has unexpectedly needed their wisdom teeth pulled, a root canal, crown, cap, or veneer can tell you dental insurance isn't a bad idea. Dental premiums are much less expensive than health insurance premiums, but most dental policies do not cover more than 80 percent of your dental services. If your company or school does not offer dental insurance, try running a search on the Internet or in your phone book for reputable providers.

Homeowner's/Renter's Insurance

If you own anything worth more than $1,000, you should probably take out a policy on the belongings in your home in case of theft or fire. To take out this type of policy, you will need to list their value. Also, make sure you photograph or film each room of your house, and keep the record in a place outside your home. If you ever do file a claim, insurance investigators may try to debate how much your belongings were worth, so it helps to have visual proof.

Any very expensive items you may own like jewelry, antiques or electronics may require separate policies and professional estimates of their worth. An insurance premium on a $10,000 wedding ring may cost more than your entire homeowner's premium! I guess it's easier to lose a ring than a house. Also, be sure to check your homeowner's or renter's policy to see if it covers your actual building structure in the event of a flood, earthquake, hurricane or other act of God. If you live in an area that is susceptible to these events, you will probably have to take out another policy to cover such incidents.

Life Insurance

Life insurance grants a specified amount of money to your designated beneficiaries in the event of your death. While life insurance policies are usually only taken out by people who have family members who depend on them—such as spouses, children, and incapacitated parents—they are cheapest for young people with no dependents (like you)! Thus, it is a great idea to start your policy now if you can get a rate that won't increase with your age or health situation.

Like all other types of insurance, you pay a premium to hold your policy, but someone else can pay that premium for you. Got any rich grandmothers? There are two kinds of policies you can take out—term life and whole life. A term life policy is for a specified amount of time, at which point you may renew it. A whole life policy lasts for your whole life (assumed to be 100 years). One benefit to having a life insurance policy is that you can arrange to borrow against it, in case you ever are feeling far from death and in the mood to install a basketball court in your backyard.

The policy owner of a life insurance policy designates the beneficiaries (the people who receive money upon your death). The policy owner does not necessarily have to be the person whose life is insured. So, watch your back if your spouse one day takes out a really large policy on you.

Disability Insurance

Most often offered by employers, this type of insurance provides a person who becomes injured or disabled on the job with the salary he would normally earn, if he's deemed incapable of continuing work duties. Trapeze artists, construction workers, and police officers should definitely consider these policies.

Long-Term Care Insurance

With the increasing costs of hospital stays and convalescent and retirement home room rentals, if you think you will be responsible for taking care of an older loved one, or just want to get a head start on the funding of your own golden years, consider paying a little bit now rather than a lot later!

A Word about Insurance Fraud

The reason insurance premiums are so high (besides the greed of the corporate world and the increasing amount of uninsured hospital visitors) is because of something called insurance fraud. Have you ever thought about how easy it would be to "pretend" your clunker was stolen, to "accidentally" drop a lit match on your living room floor, or to "slip" while on the job? Don't even think about it. Insurance companies do not just hand over a check whenever you claim you need one. Instead, they hire investigators to research all claims made, so that they are not duped by fraud.

Yup, insurance company employees are right up there with lawyers and IRS representatives, but only because they have to be. So keep your nose clean, and our premiums low!

chapter 17

Bartering, Bargaining, and Other Ways to Annoy Salespeople

How great of a shopper are you?

1. If you like a car and want to buy it, what would you tell the salesman?
    a. "I love it, I'll take it!"
    b. "So, how much is it again?"
    c. "I don't know, the other dealer is much less expensive..."

2. Financing is _____.
    a. The only way I can buy things
    b. A good way to spread out your payments
    c. Dangerous—I pay with cash

3. Bargaining is _____.
    a. For cheapskates
    b. For the old-fashioned
    c. My forte

If you scored:

Mostly a's: A salesperson's dream
Mostly b's: Not too savvy
Mostly c's: You name it, you got it!

The time will come when you are ready to buy your first new car, leather couch, or Prada purse. Before you max out your credit card, spend a few minutes reading advice that could potentially save you hundreds, or even thousands of dollars.

As a freshman, my first "large" purchase was a thirteen-inch TV/VCR. Okay, so that was back in the days of VCRs—a movie-watching machine that you have probably never even seen. But if I had been a smart shopper, I could have gotten the thing for no more than $150. But because I didn't obey any of the following rules, I spent $410! I got gypped! Many stupid purchases later, I now know how to shop.

Negotiation 101

Here are a few negotiating tips for those impulse purchases that you will later regret.

1 Never buy anything that you have not seen first. Now, it's okay to buy a shirt from *www. jcrew.com* or a costume from ebay, but do not buy a car online! I can't tell you how many times I've (not) learned this lesson. In college, there was an art student who had these amazing Rastafarian-style paintings hanging at a local club, and we asked him to come over to look at our house and paint something that would match our décor. Of course, he wanted $300 up front, but that was "a great deal," as he was selling his Bob Marley's in New York for over $1,000. Well, either my house was very uninspiring, or more likely, he just wanted to make a quick buck, because the already-paid-for painting he brought to us two days later is so pitiful, people look at it and ask me, "Did you paint that?" Yet, it still hangs on my wall to remind me of that mistake, and because I spent $300 on it!

2 Research the product. The knowledgeable consumer will always get a good deal. However, don't do your research behind a sales manager's desk. First, research the product on the Internet, in magazines, or by asking others who have already shopped for the same thing. Every store has a pitch for why their product is better. In fact, while I was recently car shopping, two different dealerships both claimed to have won the same award for service! After researching, write down the facts you learned from subjective, reliable sources, and use that to compare what you're being told by the salesperson to the truth.

3 **Shop around.** I used to work at a jewelry store, where I went through three months of sales training before selling diamonds for a year. Believe me, if there is one thing salespeople learn, it's "Don't let the customer get away." While shop-arounders are a salesperson's nightmare, they are the smartest consumers and will always get the best deal. From word of mouth, or by picking the most appealing companies online, pick three different reputable stores or dealers that sell the same product. Spend the time to hear each place's sales shpiel, then make an educated decision.

4 **Take someone with you!** The old "good cop/bad cop" scheme works wonders at furniture stores. With a friend, plan a script beforehand—and when you are nearing the purchase point, have one person say something like, "Well, it's nice, but the other one is much cheaper," or "I like the no-cost warranty the other place had." This will bring any talented salesperson to his feet and cause him to give you the best deal possible on your new living room set, because another motto of sales is "anything to make the sale." As sexist as it may sound, girls, always take a guy with you when you are buying anything electronic or motorized. And guys, always take a girl with you when you are buying jewelry or expensive clothing. When buying any used car, always take it to a mechanic before you buy it, or bring one with you. My brother recently bought a '64 Chrysler that was advertised to be in "immaculate shape." After a trip to our trusted mechanic, we returned with an estimate of $1000 of

repairs the car required to function properly. After we used that for bargaining, he got the car for almost half the asking price!

5 **Bargain.** A few years ago, I ended up in Tijuana (I got lost on my way down to San Diego—long story). Anyway, at the border, there are all these men and women out on the street trying to sell blankets, chess sets, sombreros, and other touristy-type stuff. I saw a pair of sandals I wanted that were marked as $12. I told the salesman that I really liked the sandals but I only had $3. He looked at me laughing, shook his head, and said, "No, no, senorita." I shrugged my shoulders and started to walk away. He said, "Wait, I am in a good mood and I want you to have the sandals—you may have them for $3." Yes! Until I opened my wallet and saw that all I had was a $20.

6 **Use your poker face.** When considering a large purchase, never sound too eager during your encounters with salespeople. Don't give them an easy sale, or act like you are really pleased with what they are telling you. Ask them several educated questions, based on your research of the product. When purchase time finally approaches, barter for your bargain. Unless you're at a store that does not negotiate pricing (usually clothing stores fall under this category), always make an offer a good deal lower than what the seller is asking. Support your offer with a comment like, "Well, I wasn't going to spend more than ___ hundred," or "I'd have to wait two more paychecks to get it at that price." Doing this almost guarantees you a decent counter-offer. When you think the sales person is as desperate as he's going to get, look him in the eye and say, "Is that really the best you can do for me?" Then, if you are 100 percent satisfied with the price and product, go for it.

7 **Try to avoid buying an extended warranty.** Buying an extended warranty usually just puts extra padding in the salesperson's pocket. Most new reputable products

should come with a warranty, and that should be all you need. If something does break when that warranty expires, it will probably be cheaper to pay for the repair than to buy an extended warranty. Extended warranties are generally a rip-off.

8 **Payment plans.** Most large purchases allow some sort of payment plan so you don't have to unload your life savings onto the counter. If you are offered a six, twelve, thirty-six, or other monthly payment plan, ask about the interest rate and any penalties incurred for early payoff. Then, compare the interest rates you could get from using your credit card or taking out a personal loan. Sometimes, your parents will provide the loan at a low (or non-existent) interest rate. Look for sales that advertise "same-as-cash financing," "0.0 percent APR," and "no interest loans." But before you sign any sales contract, read all the fine print, and make sure you completely understand all of the terms of payment. Once you're committed, don't miss payments, because this will seriously screw up your credit!

May you enjoy all of your large purchases! And may you not be one of those people who buys things merely for the thrill of the hunt. If you are, keep your receipts and learn the conditions of your state's "buyer's remorse" law, which most likely will allow you seventy-two hours to return your purchase if you feel you were "pressured" into buying the item. Happy Shopping!

chapter 18

Welcome to the World of Budgeters and Cheapskates

How cheap are you?

1. Tipping is _____.
    a. A fun thing to do to sleeping cows
    b. Just another way the world is trying to rip me off
    c. Customary when you receive good service

2. You walk by a homeless man. Do you open your wallet?
    a. I would if there was anything in there!
    b. Yeah, right—he'd just spend it on booze
    c. Yes, and I use the $5 to buy him a Happy Meal

3. When you go out to eat with friends, what do you order?
    a. Nothing—I usually just take a few bites from my friends' food.
    b. Water and soup—as long as the crackers come free.
    c. I start with chips and salsa, then a burger, throw in a Mud Pie, and wash it down with a shake—gotta keep this engine running!

If you scored:

Mostly a's: Beyond help.
Mostly b's: You're cheap and you know it.
Mostly c's: Living large and loving it!

Welcome to the world of budgeters and cheapskates! But don't get me wrong, neither of these titles is a bad thing—especially in this economy. In fact, they are vital roles for anyone entering the Real World who earns so little he doesn't even have to pay taxes. Whether you earn $200 a month, or $20,000 a month, it is always wise to become a connoisseur of thrift and frugality. Think of all the celebrities who were hot for five seconds but now have to go on Hollywood Squares and do infomercials because they didn't know how to follow a budget.

There have been several books published that expose the secrets of self-made millionaires, and all of them concur on one point—smart, wealthy people are not necessarily big spenders. Most drive economy cars, shop the sale rack, and don't eat out every night. So if this is the life that money gets you, why would you want to be rich? Well, you can stew over that once you've made your first million. But for now, start forming a penny-pinching mindset. This chapter will teach you how to form a simple budget and how to save money in almost every aspect of your life!

Your Fill-in-the-Blank Budget

Forming a budget is useless if you do not have a good estimate of how much you make each week or month. Give your Real World life a realistic amount of time—but not too long—to see how much you are earning and spending. After you feel you have established a financial routine, fill in these blanks.

1. How much do I earn each month, before taxes?
   Gross income: _____

2. How much do I take home after taxes?
   Net income: _____

3. How much is my rent/room and board?
    Rent: _____

4. How much are my utility bills?
    Telephone: _____
    Electricity: _____
    Gas/Water: _____
    Cable: _____
    Total: _____

5. How much do I spend on food?
    Food: _____

6. How much do I spend on toiletries/cosmetics?
    Personal Items: _____

7. How much do I spend on large bills?
    Tuition: _____
    Car Payment: _____
    Car Maintenance (gas/oil/repairs): _____
    Car Insurance: _____
    Health Insurance: _____
    Other: _____

8. How much do I spend on "fun stuff?"
    Cell Phone: _____

    Clothes: _____
    Eating Out: _____
    Entertainment: _____
    Other: _____

9. How much do I donate to charity?
    Donations: _____

10. How much do I save/invest?
    Save: _____
    Invest: _____

11. How much do I have left?
    Remainder: _____

By now, you will either be blown away by how much money you waste each month, or you will be proud of yourself for all of your frugal spending that allows you left over money to save, invest, or have fun with! Once you keep track of where your money is going, it is easy to see the differences between necessities and luxuries. Necessities are any items you can't live without. Luxuries are items that you want but don't need. If you ever get confused between the two, imagine that someone told you that you were going to be on Survivor and be taken to a deserted island, and you could only bring five things with you. What you would bring would hopefully be necessities; otherwise, good luck!

Now that you have assessed your spending, it is time to create a budget that is reasonable and allows you to live within your means. If you are in the hole every month, look at your answers and see where you can cut down, or what you can cut out altogether. Do not allow yourself to go into debt by spending money on anything that is not a necessity, no matter how much you think you may be earning next month or next year. Create your budget based on today's earnings. And when you do get a raise, don't automatically spend your extra earnings; apply them to a "smart" category, like savings or investments.

Using the following worksheet, write your net income at the top. Then, for each category, write a reasonable amount that you can abide by in the blank. As you fill in the blanks, deduct the amount budgeted from your income, and you will see directly how the money vanishes. If you find that you run out of money before you are finished, start over and cut down on your spending. You may have to get rid of your cell phone and wear last year's shoes a bit longer than planned, but it is better than going into debt. The categories are listed in a suggested order of importance. For instance, "charity" and "savings" are listed near the top, because if you make enough money to put some aside for others and for your future, those are the first and best things you should budget for to avoid feeling like you have leftover money in the end that you can spend. Charity is what makes you a decent human being. And saving money is really just paying yourself.

My Monthly Budget

Gross Income	$_____	deduct spending from income and total here
Taxes	$_____	income minus taxes total here
Charity	$_____	− _____
Savings	$_____	− _____
Rent	$_____	− _____
Food	$_____	− _____
Utilities	$_____	− _____
Insurance	$_____	− _____
Car Costs	$_____	− _____
Tuition	$_____	− _____
Other Bills	$_____	− _____
Clothing	$_____	− _____
Entertainment	$_____	− _____
Miscellaneous	$_____	− _____
Investments	$_____	− _____
	Remainder	$ _____

A Word about Taxes

Taxes are perhaps one of the hardest concepts of the Real World that you will need to understand, and it may take many years and lunch dates with CPA's to truly figure out how they work. Basically though, because you enjoy the freedoms of America, Uncle Sam wants something back. If you are an income-earning citizen, you are required to complete a tax form and return it to the IRS before April fifteenth each year. If your company automatically deducts taxes from your paycheck, you need to complete a W-2 form. Your previous year's employers should provide you a form with the annual income information you need. If you received untaxed income, you need to complete a 1099 Tax Form, stating all your income—and hopefully you have been putting money aside to pay your taxes.

If you do not make that much money, or you claim a lot of deductions (charitable contributions, large interest payments, dependents, tuition, etc.), you may receive a tax return—yup, real money! So, go ahead and file even if you don't make a lot of money. If you do not file taxes, or do not claim all of your earnings, watch out because IRS employees are sneaky little buggers. If they audit you, you could be charged, fined, and jailed! So, find an accounting student or an online program like TurboTax, and file before spring break!

Seventy-Five Ways to Save Money

At Home

*   About half of the average American's electricity bill goes toward heating and cooling—close and seal your windows and your doors when using air and heat, try to get programmable thermostats, and clean out your air ducts and vents regularly.

*   Turn your thermostats off at night—open a window if it is hot, or use an extra blanket if it is cold.

- Whenever you leave a room, turn off all the lights and electronics.

- Buy energy-efficient appliances, marked with "Energy Star."

- Get a cell phone with a better plan if you use both cell and home phones, and cancel your home phone service.

- Consider settling for "basic cable," instead of $30 worth of extra channels that you shouldn't be wasting your valuable time watching!

- Get a long distance calling card, or shop competitive rates with long distance carriers. Avoid monthly fees and any plan that costs over seven cents a minute for nation-wide long distance.

- Consider buying a house or condo instead of renting— when you own and sell, you get something back. Rent just goes down the tube!

Food

- Cook in bulk, and freeze the leftovers in small portions, creating your own microwave meals. Saves time and money!

- Prepare your meals based on things you already have and things that are on sale at the store.

- Set a meal budget, allotting so much for each meal. (e.g., $3—breakfast; $5—lunch; and $10—dinner)

- Whenever meat goes on sale, buy a reasonable amount in bulk. Package it into one-pound batches and freeze.

- When you go through a drive-thru, ask for extra sauce. Ketchup, mustard, and BBQ sauce run around $3 a bottle!

- If you find an expired item on a grocery store shelf, some stores will give you an unexpired similar product for free.

- Don't grocery shop when you are hungry—everything will look good!

- Consider online grocers—the delivery charge is still probably cheaper than the impulse buying you avoid when you don't go into the store.

- Clip coupons! Some stores will double and triple them!

- Don't use coupons just to use them. See if the store brand is cheaper.

- Only buy in bulk if you know you will eat it all before it expires.

- Comparison shop—visit three different stores, write down the prices of items you frequently buy, and start shopping at the cheapest store.

- Instead of buying Starbucks and fruit smoothies, try making your own at home!

- When eating out, order water instead of $2.50 drinks.

- Don't always offer to pick up or evenly split the tab when going out to eat with friends—pay for what you ate.

- Bring your lunch to work or school—you'll save time and money.

- Split meals with a friend at places that serve large portions.

- Despite widespread belief, sometimes eating out (fast food) is cheaper than cooking at home! So drive-thru Del Taco on "Taco Tuesday" and do good for your piggy bank.

Shopping

- Only shop when you need something, not just for fun.

- Go to the library to check out books rather than buying them all the time (except this one—you'll need your own copy of this one).

- Blockbuster is almost as expensive as a matinee! Find a drugstore, hole-in-the-wall rental place, or Red Box location with new releases for a buck.

- Whenever you feel like buying a new wardrobe, donate your old clothes to the needy—seeing their situation will make you think you "need" less (or it will at least give you a tax write-off).

- Check out websites like *www.priceline.com* and *www. cheaptickets.com* for airfare, rental cars, and other travel expenses. You may have less flexibility but also less money to pay!

- Try to avoid buying items that are "dry clean only."

- Instead of buying expensive gifts and cards, make them! Gifts from the heart and those that offer services to others are more thoughtful and less expensive.

- Check out garage sales, yard sales, and swap meets for "unique" odds and ends.

- Whenever you are considering buying something (besides food), see if it is offered on *www.ebay.com*. It probably is, and you may even find it new, for much cheaper.

- Wait for the sale! Sales are often advertised in the Sunday paper. If you just can't wait, most stores will comp you the difference within a week or two of when you bought a sale item, if you have your receipt.

- Shop with cash. Put a designated amount in an envelope each week, and don't allow yourself to pull out the plastic!

- Look high and look low on the shelves. The most expensive items are usually at eye level.

- Avoid check-out counter purchases—you know, the magazines, accessories, and other "little things" that really do cost something.

- Always put something back. If you select more than five things that you like, but don't need, do not approach the register without returning one.

- Before you consider buying something, first tally the amount of hours it will take you of working to pay it off. You may reconsider.

- Stock up on toiletries and other frequently used items when they go on sale.

- Look for rebates. The "hassle" of mailing a letter can get you a lot of cash back on electronics, DVD's and other items.

- When picking up photos, ask for your money back on poorly developed pictures.

- If an item is mistagged in a store, the store should always give you the lower price—and sometimes they'll give it to you for free.

- Before you want to buy something, give yourself a "waiting period" of twenty-four hours, or seven days, to really think about it.

- Before you buy anything, think whether you can reuse or recycle something you already have instead.

- Watch your traveling speed—you conserve fuel at lower, steady speeds, so drive the speed limit and use cruise control on highways.

- Make sure your tires are properly inflated. Too little or too much air pressure can reduce your miles per gallon.

- Lighten your load. Don't tote around wind-resistent features (sporting racks), and don't keep really heavy items in your car for a long time.

- If you will be idling for more than one minute, turn the ignition off.

- Try rolling down your windows or using your vents instead of turning on the air conditioner.

- Keep your filters clean—your fluids will last longer, and fewer car parts will need to be replaced.

- Carpool!

- When running errands, do preliminary research by phone instead of driving around, and try to run all your errands in one organized trip.

- When you buy a car, consider the resale value. Red and black cars sell easier than browns and greens.

- Don't buy new cars. As you roll off the lot, so does several grand from the resale price. Try buying cars right off a lease, instead—they should be in good condition and have low mileage.

- Buying a car rather than leasing gives you something to cash in when you are ready for a new car.

Entertainment

- Check your local movie theaters and bowling alleys for "Discount night." Sometimes, Monday, Tuesday, or Wednesday bring daily deals.

- Many museums, libraries, and festivals offer free entertainment.

- Get creative on your nights out with friends. Ice block sledding and video scavenger hunts can be fun!

School

- If money's tight, consider a community college for your general education, then transfer to a bigger school junior year.

- Buy used books; then sell them when the semester is over.

- Take advantage of free campus activities and student discounts.

- Apply for student loans, scholarships, and grants. You don't have to pay back scholarships and grants!

Health/ Beauty

- Go to a beauty school to get your haircuts, manicures, and massages. While students do perform the services, their instructors "fix" any mistakes.

- Instead of using shaving gel when shaving, try using conditioner.

- Only use a pea-sized amount of toothpaste—it adds up.

- Conserve water by turning off the faucet while brushing

your teeth, washing your face, and getting ready to get in the shower.

- Instead of buying an eyebrow brush, just spray hairspray on a cheap toothbrush.

- Lipstick can double as blush if you rub it into your fingers.

- Many store-brand facial cleansers work just as well as the expensive ones.

Bills

- Pay your bills on time to avoid late fees and interest.

- Try paying your bills online, by phone, or by using an automatic withdrawal from your account to save postage fees.

- Check out *www.lowermybills.com* for more ways to save money on phone bills, auto insurance, credit card rates, and in many other areas!

Don't waste your earning time—get started now. Save as much money as you can by following your budget and these tightwad tips. But don't be cheap in a tacky way! Never forget the importance of tipping service providers, remembering loved ones' birthdays, and making charitable contributions every once in a while. Good luck to all you future millionaires!

part 4

Surviving Physically

chapter 19

Avoiding the "Freshman Fifteen"

How "spudly" are you?

1. Your idea of a workout is _____.
    a. A trip to the fridge and back
    b. A walk to school
    c. A run to the gym, a two-hour workout,
        then a jog back home

2. The Food Pyramid is _____.
    a. Burger King's logo
    b. A bunch of fat cheerleaders doing stunts
    c. A guide to daily food choices from the
        five food groups

3. The "Freshman Fifteen" is _____.
    a. The fifteen professors I am going to
        impress
    b. The fifteen upperclassmen I want to meet
    c. The fifteen inevitable pounds I don't want
        to gain

If you scored:

Mostly a's: Couch potato
Mostly b's: Mashed potatoes and gravy
Mostly c's: Baked potato, but hold the sour cream

Did you get asked to leave the swim team because your "dives" drained the pool? Did your prom date really break his foot when you stepped on it? Do nicknames like "Tubby," "Jello Jigglers," and "Porky" bring back painful memories? Well, my Snickers-scarfing friends, it's time for revenge! While you thin out and "blossom," all of those snotty, skinny kids from high school may take a walk in your shoes once they go to college and encounter . . . The Freshman Fifteen.

The Freshman Fifteen is a term granted to college freshman, and really anyone who moves out into the Real World for the first time, and gains a little more baggage than he or she left home with. All of those toga parties, midnight taco runs, convenience foods, and cafeteria grub (hey, they don't have to tell you what's in Sunday's Surprise), makes for one very large eighteen-year-old. In fact, for many, fifteen pounds is a kind understatement. So, if you want to be recognizable (or unrecognizable if you are now pleasantly plump) at your ten-year reunion, you need to get eight hours of sleep a night and start following two key phrases that you may have ignored thus far: Eat right and Exercise!

Eat Right!

But Wendy's is so easy, Papa John's delivers, Carl's Jr. has a drive-thru. Too bad! Words like "easy," "delivers," and "drive-thru" are exactly what is causing America's intense obesity problem! While fast food and large portions are just so comfortable for emotional eaters, healthy food is what will prevent you from having to take Lipitor and wear a heart patch by the time you turn thirty. Remember that triangle filled with food your middle school science teacher busted out on the overhead to show you how much fruit and how little chocolate you really should be eating every day? If not, let's review.

There are five major food groups that are naturally good

for you before your add the fats, oils, and sweets to them. If you eat a well-balanced diet and follow the suggested serving sizes, your heart and cholesterol level will love you. So, what counts as a serving of each? For an average-sized adult:

Grains: 1 slice of bread; 1 ounce cereal (ready-to-eat); ½ cup cooked cereal, rice or pasta.

Milk: 1 cup milk or yogurt; 1 ½ ounces natural cheese; 2 ounces cheese.

Vegetables: 1 cup raw, leafy vegetables; ½ cup other vegetables—cooked/raw; ¾ cup vegetable juice.

Fruits: 1 medium-sized apple, banana, or orange; ½ cup chopped or canned fruit; ¾ cup fruit juice.

Meats and Beans Group: 2 to 3 ounces cooked lean meat, poultry, or fish; 1 cup cooked dried beans; 2 eggs; 4 tablespoons peanut butter or ²/₃ cup of nuts. (Suggested servings taken from the 2000 Dietary Guidelines of the U.S.D.A.)

Every food group provides important nutrients that your body needs. Eating too little or too much of any food can cause vitamin deficiencies or can otherwise be harmful to your health. If you are vegetarian or have other unique eating habits or allergies, you need to substitute the food groups that you are missing with a supplement. Everybody should talk with a doctor about their diet and take a multi-vitamin each day in case you do miss out on some essential vitamins. Following are some of the nutrients your body needs to function properly, and the suggested nutrient level you should be receiving, according to the government's Recommended Dietary Allowances. (Remember, RDA recommendations can vary based on your age and size.)

- **Calories:** The measurement of energy that is produced by your metabolism of food; calories need to be both consumed and burned each day. RDA: 2,000.

- **Proteins:** The building blocks, composed of amino acids, for all of your body parts. RDA: 50–60 grams

- **Fat:** Provider of energy and four vitamins (A, D, E, and K) to the body, as well as the supplier of fatty acids needed for many of your body's activities. RDA: Saturated fat, 20 grams; Total fat, 65 grams.

- **Cholesterol:** Forms vitamin D, cell membranes, and sex hormones. RDA: Less than 300 milligrams.

- **Carbohydrates:** Provide energy to your body. RDA: 300 grams.

- **Sodium:** Salts that aid in food preservation. RDA: Less than 2,400 milligrams.

- **Sugars:** A powdery substance used to sweeten foods. RDA: Less than 10 teaspoons a day (remember, sugar is added to most foods).

- **Dietary Fiber:** Adds bulk, absorbs water, and aids in eliminating waste from your intestine. RDA: 20–30 grams.

Following are some other eating habits that will ensure that you always fit through the door:

- Avoid large amounts of caffeine and alcohol.

- There is nothing beneficial about tobacco—don't smoke!

- Don't do drugs. Duh.

- Get in the habit of filling up on "European portions," which are much smaller and thus more healthy than American serving sizes.

- Eat breakfast to get your metabolism going!

- Drink lots of water—at least 64 fluid ounces a day!

- Eat slowly; you'll fill up faster.

- Eat small meals several times a day rather than three large ones.

- Snack on carrots and pretzels instead of candy and chips.

- Avoid fast food!

- Eat more fruits, vegetables, and grains, and less fat and cholesterol.

- Try not to add salt or butter to your food.

- Look for nonfat or lowfat labels on staple items like milk, cheese, meats, etc.

- Read the labels! Just what are you consuming?

- Don't eat during the two hours before bed.

- Don't clear your plate! (Mom was wrong on this one—leaving a few bites from every meal keeps a few more calories and fat grams off your gut.)

- Exercise!

Wendell Phillips said, "Health lies in labor, and there is no royal road to it but through toil." Translation: If you want a nice butt, get off your butt! Yup, you've got to work for it. Not only does exercise give you a more lusted-after physique, but it also makes you a more energetic, happy person! While the recommended amount of exercise changes with every year and every source, you will most likely improve your dating life if you shoot for thirty minutes a day, three times a week. Before you start any exercise program, always consult with a doctor. (Although 90 percent of you won't consult with a doctor, at least I'm not liable if you faint on your way into the gym.)

And no, you do not need a gym to work out! Look around you. Unless you live in Minnesota or Canada or some other place eternally devoid of warm weather, use your environment (or your living room) as your own personal gym. You may find that you enjoy the scenery of your local park or beach much more than the rear end of the person on the treadmill in front of you at 24 Hour Fitness.

Choose a form of exercise that you enjoy—if you hate jogging, you are less likely to do it. But, if you really enjoy rollerblading or tennis, you will be more apt to exercise. You can also try incorporating the mentality of fitness into your daily life. Instead of using elevators, walk. Park far away from your destination and enjoy the stroll. When you are at stoplights, do some sort of flexing with your sitting muscles. When you watch TV, do crunches. And laugh—a lot. Laughing actually burns more calories than many physical activities. Go dancing. Hiking. Skateboarding. It's not hard to find ways to exercise—without having to pop in a video.

A workout buddy is a must. Unless you have the willpower of the little engine that could, you will probably not feel like working out on a rainy day, or a cold day, or Monday, or Friday, or any other day that ends with the letters d-a-y. So, get a committed buddy to drag you out of bed and spot you if you do weight training. Also, pick a scheduled time you can really stick to—your consistency will help make exercise a priority.

When you exercise, make sure you do activities that are beneficial to both your muscles (strength training) and your heart (cardiovascular). Combine lifting weights with aerobic exercise. As you build up your muscle, you will burn even more calories, thus trimming out your waist line while forming nice abs and pecs. Remember, muscle weighs more than fat, so if you start to gain weight when you begin exercising, don't freak out and head to McDonald's. In fact, forget the scale altogether. Instead, regularly take measurements of your waist, hips, arms, and legs. Decreased measurements are proof of good work. And if you want to know how many calories are burned doing some of the most popular exercises, consult this chart, based on the approximate amount of calories burned by a person who weighs 150 pounds. (If you weigh less, you will burn fewer calories; if you weigh more, you will burn more.)

Activity	Calories Burned Per Hour
Basketball	350
Biking (10 mph)	250
Hiking	300
Racquetball	600
Rollerblading	350
Rowing	820
Running (5 mph)	700
Running (10 mph)	1200
Skiing cross-country	700
Skiing downhill	600
Soccer	550
Swimming 25 yds/min.	275
Swimming 50 yds/min.	550
Tennis	450
Walking (4 mph)	420

When you exercise, always begin by stretching, and end with a cool-down, so you don't pull your muscles. And make sure you always drink plenty of water to replenish all that dripping sweat—or "perspiration," if you're a girl. If you do not have a lot of time to exercise, try this fifteen minute work-out. To do this, you will need a chair or something to hold on to, and a soft rug or towel on the ground.

Fifteen Minute Workout

1. **Warm-up:** Starting at the top of your body, stretch every body part, working your way down. Slowly and evenly roll your neck, arms, wrists, waist and ankles in circular motions. Then, stretch your legs by standing plié style, with your legs spread wide apart from each other and your feet pointing out. Shift your body weight back and forth without letting your knees extend past your feet. Do hurdle stretches by sticking one foot out in front of your body, while keeping the other planted in back, and squat and raise up, stretching your calves. Then, bend your legs at the knee and raise them both forward and backward, supporting them with your arms.

2. **Arm workout:** Do as many push-ups as you can in one minute (shoot for ten). You can do them girl or boy style; just make sure you keep your back straight and parallel to the ground.

3. **Ab workout:** Do as many crunches as you can in one minute (shoot for fifty) by doing "half sit-ups." Remember to focus on pulling your shoulders off the ground, and not your head.

4. **Legs:** Balancing on your chair, stand plié style, and squat slowly ten times. Then, stand with your legs together, knees touching, and squat ten times. Remember to keep your back straight, and squat low to the ground.

5. **Repeat** steps 2, 3, and 4 three times, keeping your reps consistent.

6. **Cool down:** Repeat your warm up slowly to stretch out your muscles.

A Word about Eating Disorders

A frighteningly significant amount of young adults suffer from weight problems on the opposite end of the scale. Eating disorders like anorexia and bulimia, brought on by societal pressures to maintain an ideal body type, are controlling the lives of more and more youth—both female and male. People with anorexia literally starve themselves from proper nutrients by only nibbling on lowfat foods. Sufferers of bulimia make themselves throw up what they eat (binge and purge) to avoid ingesting calories. Both are mental illnesses in which the victims think they are fat, even if they are not. If you or any of your friends show symptoms of these illnesses such as frequent trips to the restroom after meals, meager nibbling, obsession over food and calories, compulsive exercising, or stress and irritability relating to food, get help! See a counselor or call a parent or a doctor—just let someone know. Although the hardest part of overcoming the illness is facing the reality of it, it is the most important step to recovery!

While there are "miracle diets," "Hollywood diets," and even "Subway diets," the simplest and safest way to maintain a healthy physique is to work for it. Take pride in your hot bod now—and when you turn fifty, you may require one less lift and tuck.

chapter 20

Pepper Spray and the Police Station:
Protect Yourself!

How street smart are you?

1. Who do you go clubbing with?
    a. Whoever's in line in front of me
    b. I go with a friend, leave with whomever
    c. A bodyguard, a bouncer, and all my best friends

2. If a new employee at your work said, "Hey, hot stuff," to you in the lunch room, you'd reply,
    a. "My coffee is hot, too."
    b. "Well, hello to you."
    c. "You want to see how heated up I can get? You will if I hear one more harassing remark out of your mouth, buddy . . ."

3. "Don't talk to strangers" is a good idea if you are
    a. In kindergarten
    b. In a dark alley
    c. Anywhere and everywhere!

If you scored:

Mostly a's: Perpetually clueless!
Mostly b's: Perpetually a target . . .
Mostly c's: Perpetually protected!

Nobody wants to be bullied, harassed, or attacked, whether you're four or forty! In fact, we don't even like to imagine the possibility of such things happening, so we often dismiss the thought of enrolling in a self-defense course or buying pepper spray. But, whether you live in Happy Valley or the 'Hood, you are always a potential victim. And the more naïve you are about the dangers lurking out yonder, the more potential you have of being a target. Protecting yourself starts with prevention, which is best done by being aware of your surroundings and knowing how to "think safe."

Through the Parking Lot and into Your Car

Whenever you head toward your car and drive home, you should be alert to your environment, even if you are a big guy with three friends, but especially if you are female and alone.

- Always know where you parked your car, and walk to it with confidence, checking your surroundings. If you have a cell phone, talk to someone for real or loudly pretend to talk to someone to ward off any attacker who wants to catch you alone.

- Always park your car in well lit, legal spaces (to avoid theft, towing, and being attacked).

- Do not get into your parked car without checking underneath and inside for unexpected passengers.

- When you walk to your car, put a key from your key ring between every two fingers or place your finger on the spray button of a bottle of pepper spray for self-defense.

- Find out where the emergency phones are located on the walk to your car, and run to one if you are approached by an attacker.

- If someone approaches you and says he needs help with a flat tire or a dead battery, or has some amazing offer of cheap merchandise in his car, boldly say you are unable to help or you are not interested, and walk in a different direction, preferably toward a crowd. Never go alone to someone else's car!

- Drive with your doors locked and windows at least three-quarters of the way rolled up to avoid carjacking.

- If someone is following you, pull into a well-lit service station or police station.

- If someone pulls up beside you and acts like something is wrong with your car, don't stop until you are in a well-lit, populated spot. (Don't worry, your car shouldn't explode before you get there.)

- If your car breaks down and you are alone, pull over, turn on your emergency lights, raise your hood, and call for help on a cell phone. If you do not have a cell phone, wait in your car with your doors locked for someone to offer to help. If someone approaches your window, only roll it down a crack and ask him or her to call for help. Do not get into that person's car, no matter how trustworthy he or she appears.

- If you are signaled by a police officer to pull over, don't roll down your windows or open the door until the officer shows you an authentic badge.

Out on the Town

It's Friday night, and you're out with a large group of friends, hanging out at your favorite club. Could you be attacked? Happens all the time.

- Use the buddy system—never go anywhere or leave anywhere alone or with someone you don't know very well.

- If you are worried, ask someone who works at your location (a club, restaurant, or even school) for an escort to your car.

- Never drive or ride with someone who has been drinking—call a cab, or pick a designated driver before you go out for the night. You don't want to be an accessory to vehicular manslaughter. Not only will it ruin someone else's life, but the guilt will devastate yours. And of course your life is endangered as well.

- Never take illegal drugs or "candy"—not only are drugs dangerous in their natural form, but you never know what they may be laced with.

- Never accept a drink from anyone who isn't an employee of an establishment or your best friend—date rape drugs are commonly slipped into drinks.

- Don't dress like a floozy, if you don't want to be treated like one. Although, someone does not have the right to touch you based on how you are dressed!

- Never trust someone you don't know based on what seems to be an innocent appearance. Crimes are still committed by people who appear pregnant, elderly, and crippled.

- Never leave a scene with someone you don't know—even if you are threatened with a weapon. Your chances of being injured are greater if you go with the person than if you run screaming from him and toward a crowd.

- Seventy-five percent of sexual assaults are committed by a person the victim knew. Though it is hard to know when you can really trust someone you think you "love," always be cautious. "No" means "no," and someone who cares about you will respect that.

- Be aware of your surroundings. Keep your distance between yourself and strangers. Call the police and report any suspicious people who appear to be lurking in areas watching people.

- Walk with confidence and speak loudly—you're less of a target if a predator thinks you will fight back.

- Enroll in a self-defense course!

Your Privacy

You don't need to become paranoid about the people around you, but it is important to protect your personal space wherever you are. Rely on your instincts. If someone is standing uncomfortably close to you—even if you are at a seemingly safe place like the library—tell him so. Don't be afraid to be assertive and say something like, "Please get away from me!" If you say this in a loud, commanding voice, no one will want to mess with you. It is better to be impolite than attacked.

Sexual Harassment

Sexual harassment occurs when any unwelcome or offensive comment, advance, or proposition of a sexual nature is made by someone in an attempt to receive a sexual favor or demean a person of less authority or power. Although our society does not tolerate sexual harassment as much as it did in the past, you may find yourself in an environment in which you feel uncomfortable because of others' behavior. It is not appropriate for someone to offer you a raise, promotion, or better grade if you "make it up to them." It is not appropriate for people to circulate sexist email, text messages, or jokes, or to hang offensive pictures on the wall of a public place. And it is not appropriate for anyone to touch you in an unwelcome way.

Sexual harassment is a sick crime, committed by egotistical, sexist people, and should not be tolerated. If you fall victim to it, tell the perpetrator that the said behavior is inappropriate, and you feel that he or she is sexually harassing you and you are not afraid to report it. That should stop the person, but if not, report the incidents to a trusted superior, and to the police, if no one else will listen. It is important that you have documented any instances, and if possible, that you have witnesses to the behavior.

Self Defense

People who physically or sexually assault others are evil criminals who use their physical power to abuse their victims. Often, they do not just want sex or money or your jewelry; they want the power of knowing they somehow "conquered" you. Because these people are not reasonable and are often acting on a drug high or extreme adrenaline rush, they are very dangerous.

The way in which you defend yourself from a possible attacker will be based on the situation, your personality, the attacker's personality and your self-defense training. I am not even going to pretend I know what is best for all of these factors in a given situation, but I do know that everyone should gain some professional training in what to do if attacked. Hopefully, you will follow the aforementioned prevention tips and have the luck of never facing an attacker, but it is always better to be prepared. Check with your local community center about a self-defense or martial arts course you can take. There are some very effective "Rape Escape" videos available online at *www.defendu.com.* But in the meantime, consider these defenses:

- Create a scene. Kick, scream, honk your horn, yell "Fire!"—anything to attract attention.

- Run as fast as you can, as far as you can. The more time and space you put between you two, the better your chances the attacker will give up.

- Try talking to stall for time to look for an escape.

- If you try to fight back, be quick and determined. You can possibly disable your attacker by strongly kicking or punching the attacker in his eyes, throat, groin or knees. Then, run!

- You can always try the "Crazy Defense." Pretending you are mentally unstable can make even an attacker a little wary.

- Remember your priorities. Is your wallet more important than your life? Follow your instincts and do what you need to stay alive.

- If you are attacked (or even if someone attempts an attack), mentally take notes of the person's description. Look for height, weight, race, age, hair and eye color, clothing, car or house descriptions, and any identifying marks such as scars, piercings, and tattoos.

After an Attack

I sincerely hope you never have to read this section because you were attacked. But if you are, immediately remove yourself from the person or scene. Do not shower, comb your hair, change your clothes, or clean any part of your body, so that the authorities can collect any evidence left in the form of clothing fibers, hairs, saliva, or semen. Contact someone you trust to support you, or call a hotline to talk with a counselor for support such as the Rape, Abuse, and Incest National Network (1-800-656-HOPE). Then, go to a hospital, where you can be examined and the police will be called to file a report.

Let the police know of any potential witnesses to your attack or physical descriptions of your attacker. If you were raped, you will need to be tested for any sexually transmitted diseases or pregnancy. Even if you were assaulted by someone you know (and maybe even love) and do not want to turn him in, do it anyway. If you don't, there is a good chance someone else will have to endure what you did. Never feel guilty if you are attacked. It is never your fault. Don't replay the situation and try to figure out what you could have done differently. You did the best you could to survive. The best thing you can do now is to cooperate with the proper authorities to capture the criminal who hurt you and prevent him from hurting someone else!

chapter 21

Call Mom, or Call 911?
How to Handle Aches and Pains

Could you survive medical school?

1. Help! Call 911! I just . . .
    a. Cut my leg shaving
    b. Twisted my ankle
    c. Cut off my leg

2. "Stop, drop, and roll" is what you do when
    a. You are teaching a dog a new trick
    b. You meet a cute member of the opposite sex
    c. You are engulfed in flames

3. Your most feared "kissing disease" is
    a. Cooties
    b. Cold sores
    c. Mono

If you scored:

Mostly a's: Try another field.
Mostly b's: Maybe consider nursing.
Mostly c's: Brain surgeon!

Never will the phrase "There's no place like home" be more appropriate than the first time you are away from Mommy and you get a boo-boo, a tummy ache, or something worse. It is amazing how immediately infantile a grown person becomes the minute he requires a thermometer or a cast. While you can call home for sympathy, it would be worth your while to learn what to do when the "bugs" infect you.

Whenever you move to a new location, you will want to choose a doctor, a dentist, and any other specialists you regularly see, so if an emergency does arise, you aren't stuck thumbing through the phone book. The first step to finding your doctors is to check with your insurance company to see whom they approve. Then, ask your friends and neighbors whom they recommend. If you ever need to see a specialist, your insurance may require you to obtain a referral first from your primary insurance. Unfortunately, based upon your insurance plan, you may not be entirely in charge of your healthcare.

Ask any potential doctors if you can first do a consultation interview. Even if you see a doctor once, you can still switch to someone else if you are not comfortable with the first doctor. During a consultation with a doctor, dentist, or specialist, check to see that the physician's personality clicks with yours. Make sure your doctor is conveniently located near you, takes the time and interest to answer all of your questions, will see you in an emergency, and doesn't regularly make you wait more than half an hour when you have a scheduled appointment. Following are the doctors you will want to see regularly, if your health requires:

General Health, Yearly Physicals, Minor Illnesses and Concerns. Primary Care Physicians, like Family Practitioners (M.D.), Internists, or Nurse Practitioners. *For annual physicals and when you need a prescription or become ill.*

Dental Work. D.D.S. (dentist) or Oral Surgeon. *For cleaning and checkups twice a year; toothache or dental needs.*

Female Reproductive System/Pregnancy. Gynecologist or OBGYN. *Annual visits once a female turns 18, or becomes sexually active or pregnant.*

Vision Problems. Optometrist (Eye Doctor). *If you have blurry or problematic vision.*

Skin Rashes or Problems. Dermatologist. *If you have sensitive skin, frequent rashes or redness, strange marks or moles, or acne concerns.*

Back or Bodily Pain. Chiropractor. *Frequent back or neck pain and tension or adjustment problems.*

Besides primary physicians and other commonly visited doctors, there is a variety of specialists you may be referred to, if you have a special situation or illness. Or, if you are considering becoming a doctor and you really want to go to school for an extra century to specialize in something, here are the fields in which you can make the big bucks!

Specialist	Scope of Specialty
Adolescent Medicine	Adolescent diagnosis and treatment
Allergy	Allergic conditions/asthma
Anesthesiology	Pain-relief during surgery
Cardiology	Heart and its functions
Ear, Nose and Throat	Disorders of the ears, nose and throat
Emergency Medicine	Emergency Room doctors/surgeons
Endocrinology	Treatment of the ductless glands
Gastroenterology	Treatment of stomach/intestine
Geriatrics	Treatment of the elderly
Hematology	Blood disorders
Immunology	The body's cellular response to disease
Infectious Disease	Acute and chronic infectious disorders
Neonatal/Perinatal	Treatment of unborn/premature babies
Nephrology	Kidney disorders
Neurology	Disorders of the nervous system

Nuclear Medicine	Radioactive treatment of disorders
Obstetrics	Pregnancy/childbirth
Oncology	Cancer treatment
Ophthalmology	Eye disorders and diseases
Pathology	Body tissue and fluids
Physical Therapy	Treatment of injury or disease recovery
Podiatry	Human foot
Psychiatry	Mental problems
Pulmonary Diseases	Treatment of lung problems
Radiology	X-rays and radioactive materials
Rheumatology	Arthritis and rheumatic disorders
Surgery	Perform surgery (several types)

Now you know who you're seeing when your doctor gives you a referral. But as far as self-diagnosing the daily bugs, viruses, and injuries you may encounter, here is a guide to twenty-five common situations you may find yourself in, including their symptoms and treatments.

DISCLAIMER: I am not a doctor, never have been, and most likely never will be one. I do not look like a doctor, act like a doctor, or think like a doctor—although my handwriting is similar to a doctor's. The following information is taken from medical journals and websites, and is only suggestive in its nature. If you are ever in doubt about how to handle someone's health, call your doctor. This is for your entertainment only (because reading about sickness and disease is just so much fun).

- **Allergies:** sensitivity to allergens, whether environmental, food, or animals. Symptoms—chronic sneezing, runny nose, watery eyes, rash, itchy throat, eyes, or nose, stuffiness. Treatment—(mild) over-the-counter allergy medicine; (more severe) see your doctor for a prescription.

- **Appendicitis:** if your appendix becomes infected, it can rupture. Symptoms—severe abdominal pain or stiffness in the lower right side, fever, nausea, loss of appetite, high white blood cell count. Treatment—immediately go to the hospital for removal surgery!

- **Asthma:** a chronic lung disease that causes breathing problems. Symptoms—wheezing, frequent coughing, shortness of breath, tightness in chest. Treatment—see a doctor (maybe for an inhaler); watch for triggers and condition yourself; don't smoke!

- **Broken Bones:** a fracture in your bone brought on by a fall or impact. Symptoms—pain from injury that persists longer than thirty minutes; see/hear a crack. Treatment—if in the neck or spine, do not move at all—call 911; otherwise, try to avoid moving the bone and go to an urgent care or emergency center for the bone to be set and stabilized.

- **Burns:** the skin comes in harmful contact with heat, fire, chemicals, or electricity. Symptoms—exposure to heat, fire, chemicals, or electricity causing a red, white, or blue color on the skin, blisters, oozing of pus, or removal of skin. Treatment—*Chemical burns:* call 911 and flush with water for forty-five minutes. *Electrical burns:* call 911, disconnect the source and remove victim from the source; if unconscious, administer CPR. *Heat/fire burns:* first degree (redness, pain, swelling)—cool the surface with water and aloe vera and apply a bandage, take pain reliever; second degree (top layer of skin burned off, second layer burned, blisters, splotchy appearance)—for mild second degree, follow steps for first degree, but for more severe burns, get medical attention; third degree (all skin layers burnt, even charred or dried white to muscles and bones)—don't remove connected clothing layers, cover area with a sterile cloth, and seek medical attention immediately.

- **Choking:** when an obstruction is blocking a person's breathing passageway. Symptoms—turning blue, no sound coming from mouth, unconscious. Treatment—If conscious, try to finger sweep item from person's throat; if not possible, give four back blows between the shoulder blades. If still choking, administer Heimlich maneuver (for adults) by standing behind victim and placing your arms around his waist with a fist below his sternum, thrust inward about two inches; if unconscious, do a finger sweep, administer CPR and call 911.

- **Cold:** a common, contagious infection. Symptoms—sore throat, congestion, coughing, sneezing, runny nose, fever. Treatment—rest, fluids, and an over the counter cold medicine should relieve symptoms. See a doctor if your nasal discharge or congestion worsens or you cough up colored mucus or blood.

- **Depression:** a mental illness causing extreme sadness or lethargy. Symptoms—any of the following for more than two weeks: depressed mood; loss of interest, pleasure, or appetite; extreme weight loss or gain; loss of energy; agitation; indecisiveness; thoughts of death or suicide; insomnia. Treatment—Talk to a doctor, therapist, or counselor immediately. They can prescribe anti-depressants.

- **Drug Overdose:** when more than the prescribed amount of prescription drugs, or a large amount of illegal drugs are snorted, consumed orally, or injected through the bloodstream. Symptoms—drowsiness or unconsciousness after a person takes a drug. Treatment—seek medical attention immediately. If the person is conscious, induce vomiting with ipecac syrup; if unconscious, begin CPR.

- **Flu:** a contagious viral infection common in flu season. Symptoms—cold symptoms, diarrhea, vomiting, cramping, aches and pains, weakness, dizziness, swollen glands, lack of appetite. Treatment—prevent the flu by getting a flu shot; rest and fluids and over-the-counter flu medicine (there is a prescription medicine that can stop the flu if caught in the first three days; see your doctor).

- **Food Poisoning:** sickness caused by ingesting contaminated or rotten food. Symptoms—severe stomach pains, vomiting, diarrhea for a day. Treatment—sip water, don't eat heavily. If severe (abdominal pain, fever, very frequent diarrhea), or continuing for more than two days, it could be botulism—seek medical attention immediately (and try to bring the food in with you).

- **Frostbite:** a condition in which body parts are exposed to intense cold. Symptoms—frozen numb extremities that have turned white. Treatment—don't rub or place in hot water; instead, place in lukewarm water or in a warm area (like under your armpits); get medical attention.

- **Fungal Skin Infection:** fungal growth on skin that is frequently exposed to dampness (athlete's foot). Symptoms—redness, cracked peeling skin, itching, burning, stinging pain, thick scaly skin. Treatment—keep area dry with powder, change socks frequently, wear shower shoes, over-the-counter medication; if serious, consult a doctor.

- **Headache/Migraine:** a tightening, constricting sensation in your head. Symptoms—tension, pressure in the head; for migraines—vomiting or nausea. Treatment—over-the-counter pain reliever; if serious or frequent, consult a doctor.

- **Mononucleosis:** "kissing disease;" a glandular fever that affects blood cells and lasts for a long time. Symptoms—extreme fatigue, fever, sore throat, enlarged lymph nodes and spleen, nausea, jaundice, headache, difficulty breathing, loss of appetite, weakness. Treatment—consult a doctor, get lots of rest and drink fluids.

- **Open Wounds:** cuts to the skin's surface that produce blood. Symptoms—a puncture, abrasion, or other cut to skin. Treatment—if mild, straight and shallow: clean the area, apply Neosporin, and apply a bandage; if more severe, seek medical attention for stitches, a butterfly bandage or sealing "glue."

- **Pink Eye (conjunctivitis):** a contagious infection of the eye. Symptoms—a pink, red or crusty eye, swelling of eyelid, blurry vision. Treatment—see a doctor for medication, don't touch anything without washing hands first to avoid spreading to your other eye or to someone else.

- **Pregnancy:** if you don't know what this is, you're not ready for the Real World! Symptoms—late period, nausea/vomiting, swollen breasts, appetite change. Treatment—see a doctor soon to begin prenatal care; take prenatal vitamins, eat healthfully, get plenty of rest, and avoid risky activities.

- **Pneumonia:** a bacteria that infects a weakened body. Symptoms—shaking chills, chattering teeth, severe chest pain, cough that brings up mucus, high temperature, profuse sweating, rapid breathing, confusion. Treatment—see a doctor for medication; early treatment may prevent a relapse.

- **Shingles:** a reoccurrence of the same virus that causes chicken pox. Symptoms—painful, burning, uncomfortable area of body that forms a rash or blistery bumps and that remains painful afterwards; sometimes caused by stress. Treatment—see a doctor for medication; if severe, you may need an IV.

- **Sinusitis:** swelling and blockage of the tissues and sinuses. Symptoms—stuffiness, congestion, drippy nose, headaches, sometimes coughing. Treatment—if occasional or mild, over-the-counter medicine; if chronic, consult a doctor for medicine or possibly nasal surgery.

- **Sleep Problems:** difficulty sleeping (insomnia) or chronic fatigue or snoring. Symptoms—trouble sleeping at night, frequent snoring, extreme lethargy. Treatment—see a doctor to diagnose the exact problem; try adjusting sleeping habits, environment, or distractions (TV, caffeine, etc.).

- **STD's:** sexually transmitted diseases such as chlamydia, herpes, hepatitis, HIV/AIDS, gonorrhea, genital warts, syphilis. Symptoms—pain, rash, swelling, or redness in the vaginal area or penis, unusual discharge, sores or lesions, unusual bleeding, pelvic pain, burning while urinating. Treatment—see a doctor immediately! STD's can be fatal, so treat them early; limit your sex partners (or abstain altogether), and always use a latex condom.

- **Strep Throat:** painful infection in the throat. Symptoms— extreme sore throat, painful swallowing, fever, fatigue, swollen lymph glands, chills. Treatment—see a doctor to get a throat culture and an antibiotic prescription.

- **Tooth Ache/Pain:** severe pain in the mouth or tooth. Symptoms—shooting pain, difficulty eating, sensitivity to hot and cold. Treatment—See a dentist and have fun at your root canal!

- **Toxic Shock Syndrome:** an infection usually caused by improper tampon use. Symptoms—fever, vomiting, diarrhea, headache, or rash on palms or soles following tampon use. Treatment—see a doctor immediately. T.S.S moves rapidly and can be fatal.

- **Unconsciousness:** when a person stops breathing. Symptoms—Person is unconscious/ does not respond, has no pulse, lips are blue. Treatment—Take a CPR class! Until then, call for help (911) first and then perform the following, if you feel comfortable that you won't hurt the person. Open the person's airway and check for breathing—

if throat is constricted, do a finger sweep. (For adults) Plug the nose, and give two full breaths, watching to see that the chest rises. (If not, retilt and try again.) Check for pulse; if none, begin chest compressions. Kneel beside victim and lace your fingers of your hands together, one on top of the other. Place your bottom fist two inches below the sternum and give fifteen compressions, smoothly pushing down about one-and-a-half to two inches. Give two more slow breaths and repeat cycle until person regains consciousness or help arrives.

- **Urinary Tract Infection:** a bacterial infection of the urinary system. Symptoms—burning while urinating, frequent need to urinate but trouble doing it, cloudy or bloody urine, sick feeling/fever. Treatment—Drink lots of fluids (cranberry juice is helpful), and see a doctor for an antibiotic.

- **Yeast Infection**—a bacterial infection in the vaginal area. Symptoms—smelly discharge, itching and burning. Treatment—see a doctor for a prescription for an oral medicine or topical cream.

chapter 22

The Difference Between Barbecuing and Boiling—and Other Cooking Basics

What kind of cookies are you serving?

1.   What do you preheat?
      a.   My flat iron
      b.   My temper
      c.   My oven

2.   A mixer is _____.
      a.   A coed party
      b.   That thing that makes coffee
      c.   An electric appliance used when baking

3.   When you hear the phrase "golden brown," you think of _____.
      a.   The ideal hair color
      b.   A nice tan
      c.   The color of the edges of a perfect cookie.

If you scored:

Mostly a's: Oreo's
Mostly b's: Pillsbury Ready-Bake
Mostly c's: Homemade Nestle Toll House

Okay, it's time to put on an apron—or figure out what one is—if you haven't yet used your kitchen for anything besides microwaving. Everyone's looking for someone special to cook them a romantic dinner. If you can't avoid the "freshman fifteen" or master the hygiene concepts, you can make up for it with your amazing culinary skills! Most people do not learn how to cook until they leave home, so you're not too far behind. But the sooner you learn now, the better you'll be eating and entertaining! Even if you are just making a tuna fish sandwich, you need to follow these cooking safety rules:

- **Wash up.** Wash your hands with soap and warm water before touching food, and after touching any type of raw meat. Also, keep your cooking surfaces (counters and sinks) clean, because if your raw poultry juice mixes with your dough, you'll wind up with Salmonella Bread!

- **Keep hot foods hot and cold foods cold.** Anything that says "keep refrigerated" on the label belongs—guess where? In the fridge. Make sure you cook your meats to the right temperature, and refrigerate all perishable leftovers.

- **Watch your expiration dates!** Guess what color ketchup turns when it's been in the cupboard for six years? I'll let you figure it out for your next science experiment. Do not consume any dairy products after a week following their sell-by date. (Just to be safe, smell products before consuming them, if you are unsure of their freshness.)

Okay, now that you are as cautious as Betty Crocker, let's check your cupboards for the basic supplies all kitchens need. Every cook should have:

Measuring cups	Measuring Spoons
Mixing Bowls	Electric Mixer

Mixing Spoons	Wire Whisk
Frying Pan	Sauce Pans
9" x 13" Baking Dish	Cookie Sheet
Casserole Dish	Blender
Muffin Pan	Can and Bottle Opener
Chef's Knife	Spatula
Meat Thermometer	Grater
Timer	Kitchen Scissors
Cutting Board	Strainer/Colander
Peeler	Cooling Rack
Rolling Pin	Ladle

And anything else you get swindled into buying at a Pampered Chef party!

If you are used to buying everything ready-made, you may be confused when you first look at a recipe. So what's a recipe? No, it's not the slip of paper that the grocery clerk hands you after you buy something—that's a receipt. A recipe will have a list of ingredients and the measurement required of them to make a food item. If you are doubling, or even tripling your recipe when you are cooking for a large crowd, you will need to double and triple the measurements. And you thought you were done with math! If your recipe has foreign words on it, welcome to the metric system—used worldwide except in America, for our convenience. In case you didn't learn it in high school, here are some of the most common measurements and their equivalents:

1 Tablespoon = 3 teaspoons   1 liter = 1 quart

4 Tablespoons = ¼ cup   1 ounce = 28 grams

8 fluid ounces = 1 cup   2 cups = 1 pint

2 pints = 1 quart   4 quarts = 1 gallon

1 quart = 1 liter   1 cup = 240 milliliters

Sorry, but you're going to have to do the math yourself on anything more complicated than that. When you step foot into the kitchen with your recipe, there are ways to make your cooking process more convenient. Follow these quick tips:

- Preheat your oven before you prepare the food to be placed in it, so you don't have to wait another fifteen minutes for the oven to heat.

- If you are cooking for guests, prep your foods before-hand, so you are not running around like the Mad Chef when everyone shows up. You can mix a casserole, make a pie, and chop the vegetables earlier in the day. Just heat what's necessary when it's time to eat!

- Overlap the preparation of your separate courses. Don't just sit there, watching your potatoes boil. Grab a cutting board and chop the meat!

- Buy your meat boneless and skinless. Though it's more expensive, the convenience is worth it!

- Buy ready-made foods. There's no rule that says you have to grate your own cheese or peel your own carrots. Buy foods labeled with "Quick fix," "Easy dinner," etc.

- Potluck! The ultimate answer to dining convenience. Assign every guest a course, and mentally rate each person's cooking ability.

And now, it's time for our cooking vocabulary lesson! Not only is your recipe going to be filled with measurements and ingredients, but there will be some instructions as well,

filled with code words, such as "sauté" and "simmer." If
you get stumped, following is your cooking glossary.

Terms	Definitions
Bake	to cook food using the dry heat of an oven
Barbecue	to cook food from an open heat source
Baste	to moisten foods with sauce to prevent dryness
Beat	to mix rapidly with a wire whisk or mixer
Blacken	to char meat over high heat in a skillet until blackened
Blend	to combine ingredients until smooth
Boil	to cook food in a bubbling liquid
Braise	to brown meat, and then cook it in a liquid
Broil	to cook rapidly, using a heat source from above
Brown	to cook food to develop an appealing color
Chill	to cool a food to below room temperature
Coat	to evenly cover food with crumbs or batter
Dash	a measurement equivalent to $1/16$ tsp.
Dice	to cut into uniform pieces
Frosting	a thick, creamy layer on top of baked goods
Fry	to cook food in hot cooking oil or fat
Grate	to rub food across a grating surface to make little pieces
Icing	a thin, creamy layer on top of a baked good
Knead	to massage dough with hands until smooth
Mash	to press or beat food until smooth
Melt	to heat a solid until it liquefies
Mix	to stir or beat two or more foods together until combined
Pinch	a measurement that is literally a "pinch" of a spice or herb
Poach	to cook a food by submerging in a simmering liquid
Puree	to change a solid food into a liquid by using a mixer

Rise	to allow a food to rise to a designated size
Roast	to cook uncovered in an oven's dry heat
Sauté	to cook a food in a small amount of butter or fat
Simmer	to cook in a liquid that is just below boiling
Steam	to cook in the vapor that is given off by boiling water
Stew	to cook a food in a pot (usually meat and vegetables)
Stir-fry	an Oriental way of cooking small pieces of food in a wok
Toast	to heat food in an oven until browned
Whip	to beat food lightly with a whisk
Zest	the colored portion of a fruit's peel; when finely grated, it is used for flavor

Okay, you are now ready to host your first luncheon or dinner party! But what are you going to serve? Depends on how much time you want to put in to it, and what level of difficulty you want to achieve (the more difficult, the more impressive). So, here are three sample menus for breakfast, lunch, and dinner. Each is marked with its accompanying level of difficulty on a scale of 1 to 10 (1= easy, 10 = difficult) as well as the time it takes to make. Enjoy!

Breakfast

French Toast (Difficulty Level: 2)
Time to Prepare: 10 minutes   Serves: 2

6 slices of French bread   *4 eggs*
½ cup of milk   *1 teaspoon cinnamon*
½ teaspoon vanilla   *powdered sugar*
syrup   *fresh berries (optional)*

Directions:
1. Grease the bottom of a skillet and heat on medium.
2. Mix eggs, milk, vanilla, and cinnamon in a dish large enough to dip the bread slices in.
3. Dip the bread slices into the mixture, soaking both sides until saturated.
4. Place the slices in the skillet and heat on each side until moisture is absorbed and slices are golden brown. Serve hot with powdered sugar, syrup, and berries.

Omelet (Difficulty Level: 5)
Time to Prepare: 20 minutes   Serves: 1

2 eggs
1 tablespoon milk
¼ cup cubed cooked ham cubes
¼ cup sliced mushrooms

1 tablespoon olive oil
¼ cup chopped green onions
salt and pepper, to taste
¹/₃ cup grated cheddar cheese

Directions:
1. In a skillet over medium heat, pour in olive oil and stir in ham, onions and mushrooms. Heat until mushrooms are tender.
2. In a bowl, combine the eggs, milk, and salt and pepper and beat with a fork.
3. Add the egg mixture to the skillet and cook on medium heat.
4. When the eggs start to set, lift the edges with a spatula, and flip it over.
5. Cook for about a minute until the omelet is set. It should look like an egg pancake. Sprinkle the cheese on one-half of the omelet, then fold it over.

234 • Real World 101

Crepes (Difficulty Level: 6)
Time to prepare: 20 minutes   Serves: 3 (9 crepes)

1 egg   *¾ cup milk*
½ cup flour   *½ tablespoon vegetable oil*
1 tablespoon sugar (sweet crepes)
* or dash of salt (savory crepes)*
Toppings: (sweet) berries, bananas, whip cream, jelly, chocolate,
caramel, powdered sugar, ice cream, peanut butter; (savory) butter,
ham, chicken, cheese, vegetables, etc.

Directions:
1. Combine all ingredients besides the toppings and beat until well mixed.
2. Heat a six-inch skillet, and spoon in $1/8$ cup batter. Lift and tilt the skillet all around to spread the crepe until it looks like a thin pancake.
3. Heat on one side until lightly browned, then heat on the other side for ten seconds. Remove from heat and stack on a plate, with paper towels in between.
4. Serve warm with toppings. (You can freeze leftovers.)

Lunch

Grilled Cheese (Difficulty Level: 2)
Time to Prepare: 5 minutes   Makes: 1 sandwich

2 slices of sourdough bread   *½ tablespoon butter*
sliced cheese (cheddar or Jack)

Directions:
1. Heat a skillet on medium heat.
2. Spread butter on one side of each slice of bread.
3. Put a slice of cheese in between unbuttered sides of bread to make a sandwich. Cook in skillet on each side until golden brown, and cheese is melted.

White Bean Soup (Difficulty Level: 5)
Time to Prepare: 40 minutes   Serves: 4

2 cans white beans   *2 chicken breasts*
2 cans shuepeg (white) corn   *1/2 yellow onion*
2 cans chicken broth   *1 can green chiles*

Directions:
1. Cook chicken in a skillet or pot of boiling water until center is white. Slice or shred into small pieces. Chop onion.
2. Put chicken, corn, beans, onion and water in a pot and cook on medium heat for 20–30 minutes, stirring often. (Or cook in a crock pot for several hours on low heat.)
3. Add a slice of cheese to each bowl of soup for flavor. Serve with French bread.

Chicken and Broccoli Fettucine
(Difficulty Level: 7)
Time to Prepare: 30 minutes   Serves: 6

1 pkg. fettuccine noodles   *1 jar alfredo sauce*
1 lb. chicken tenders   *1 head of broccoli*

Directions:
1. Fill a pot with water and boil. Add chicken tenders and cook until done. Slice in small pieces. (Or buy chicken already cooked to save time.)
2. Chop and steam the broccoli in a vegetable steamer or pan of water until slightly tender.
3. Boil another pot of water and add the fettuccine noodles with a little salt. Cook, stirring occasionally, for 5–8 minutes, or until desired tenderness.
4. Drain the noodles and return to pot. Mix in sauce, broccoli, and chicken and cook, stirring often on low-medium heat for 10 minutes. Serve!

Dinner

Salmon Steaks (Difficulty Level: 5)
Time to Prepare: marinate 30 min., cook 30 min.
Serves: 4

1 pound fresh salmon
1 tablespoon vegetable oil
1 tablespoon Worcestershire sauce

¼ cup lemon juice
1 tablespoon water
1 teaspoon minced garlic

Directions:
1. Rinse salmon and cut into four serving sizes.
2. In a dish, combine lemon juice, vegetable oil, water, Worcestershire sauce, and garlic. Place the salmon in the dish, and turn it on both sides to coat.
3. Cover and marinate at room temperature for 30 minutes (if you marinate any longer, stick it in the fridge).
4. Turn your oven to broil. Place fish on a broiler pan, and broil on the highest rack for 5 minutes. Turn the salmon over and brush with the marinade. Broil for 4–8 minutes longer or until the salmon flakes when sliced with a fork.

Mexican Lasagna (Difficulty Level: 7)
Time to Prepare: 1 hour   Serves: 8

10 flour tortillas
2 cups grated Mexican cheese
1 large can enchilada sauce
1 can black olives

4 chicken breasts
2 cans black beans
1 can chiles
1 box Spanish rice

Directions:
1. Cook Spanish rice according to directions on box.
2. Cook chicken in a pot of boiling water until white in center. Shred into small pieces and place in a bowl. Stir in enchilada sauce.
3. In a 9"x13" baking dish, overlap 3 tortillas to layer

the bottom. Divide all the ingredients into thirds and add them to "lasagna" in three layers in this order: beans, chicken in sauce, rice, chiles, olives, cheese, then tortillas. (But, don't place tortillas on top layer of casserole.)
4. Bake in a preheated oven at 350 degrees for 30-40 minutes. Serve with sour cream and/ or salsa.

Stuffed Beef Tenderloin (Difficulty Level: 9)
Time to Prepare: 1 hour   Serves: 4–5

2 lbs. beef tenderloin   ¼ cup seasoned bread crumbs
1 sm. pkg. frozen spinach   2 tablespoons butter
1 tablespoon olive oil   1 tablespoon minced garlic
½ cup mozzarella cheese

Directions:
1. Defrost the frozen spinach according to the instructions, and make sure it is shredded into small pieces.
2. Heat the olive oil on medium heat in a skillet and add the spinach, stirring until well saturated.
3. Pound out the beef tenderloin. In a line down the center, spread the spinach. Sprinkle the cheese on top of the spinach, and roll the tenderloin to look like a snail's shell. If necessary, tack with toothpicks.
4. Melt the butter in a small dish, and add in the bread crumbs and garlic. Coat the tenderloin roll in the crust mixture with your hands.
5. Bake in a 400 degree preheated oven for 15–20 minutes, or until desired doneness. Slice into 1-inch pieces and serve.

Add a couple of side dishes to these recipes and *voila!* Your friends will deem your place the permanent location for Sunday dinner. But, if you still can't master the art of kneading mid-recipe, call your home-base chef. That's what moms are for!

chapter 23

Where Do They Keep the Nutmeg?
And What's Nutmeg?

How great of a grocery shopper are you?

1. Coupon clipping is for:
    a. Bored housewives
    b. Tightwads
    c. Anyone with common sense!

2. At your store, the "deli" is located:
    a. Next door, at Subway.
    b. Near the back?
    c. Through the right entrance and twenty steps northeast

3. Your "staples" are:
    a. In your stapler
    b. Chips and drinks
    c. Bread, milk, butter and eggs

If you scored:
Mostly a's: Let your roomies do your shopping!
Mostly b's: Stick to eating out.
Mostly c's: Can you pick up a few things for me?

While your great new apartment may come with cable, a microwave, and a refrigerator, it will not come with free food. Some of the harshest realities a young adult will face living on his own is how quickly food runs out, and even worse—how expensive it is. Don't get discouraged, hungry friends; learning a few lessons about grocery shopping will make it more affordable, and yes, even enjoyable.

Making a List

Remember how much fun it was riding in the cart with Mom when you were four, swiping boxes of sugar-filled cereal off the shelves and hiding them underneath the dog food so she wouldn't notice them until they were paid for? Well, now you can buy as much junk as you want to! But a few days of Cheetos, Ding Dongs, and ice cream is all you'll need to know why the food pyramid was created.

In case you sat next to the school hottie in science class, let's review. There are five basic food groups from which you should have a certain number of servings each day: dairy, protein, grains, fruits and vegetables. It is quite possible to combine all the food groups into one meal. Take for instance, pizza. If you were to eat a slice of sausage and green peppers with cheese and marinara on bread dough, then you've successfully consumed a balanced meal. But, I would not suggest eating pizza three times a day. (For more on that, re-read "Avoiding the Freshman Fifteen.")

So basically, you're going to want to get a variety of foods that will be both nutritious and appetizing. No matter how healthy the makers of Tofurky claim it is, if you don't like the Tofurky taste, it will wind up in the garbage can. So, don't plan on buying things you don't eat. To organize your grocery purchases, make a list—yes, even if you're a guy. Guys like to eat, so spending a couple of minutes before you head to the store thinking about what you like to eat shouldn't be too painful. It's best to keep your list posted somewhere easy to find, like on your refrigerator, so whenever you realize you ran out of milk or that you need batteries, you can just jot down the item you need before you forget.

The first time you go grocery shopping, you're going to need to stock up on all kinds of things you never even realized your parents bought. It's good to get all these basics during your first big shopping expedition, especially if Dad's coming along with his credit card. Most of these items don't expire and will one day be needed.

Walk around each room of your place beforehand and think of every possible thing you may need—and add it to your list. Consider the following for the areas of your house:

- **Apartment or living quarters:** light bulbs, paper towels, cleaning supplies for both your house and your clothes, napkins, a broom, dust pan, mop, garbage bags, dish soap, fire extinguisher, batteries and flashlight

- **Medicine cabinet:** Band-Aids, cough syrup, rubbing alcohol, Pepto Bismol, and aspirin or headache-relieving medicine (you're sure to need some)

- **Bathroom:** soap, shampoo, conditioner, a razor, deodorant, lotion, toothbrush, toothpaste, dental floss, comb/ brush, hair sprays and gels, and cosmetics

- **Refrigerator door:** ketchup, mustard, mayonnaise, butter, barbecue sauce, salad dressing, salsa, and a cute magnet.

- **Baking cupboard:** salt, pepper, flour, sugar, vegetable oil, brown sugar, powdered sugar, yeast, cinnamon, vanilla extract, and any spices you like to use.

Once you've gotten all the basics out of the way, it's time to get down to the good stuff—food! If you like to cook, write down a few meals that you would enjoy eating, then itemize the foods you need to make each meal. If you prefer ready-made foods, such as the stuff you find in the frozen foods section, write down Dino nuggets and taquitos. And, don't forget a few fresh staple items like bread, eggs, milk, cereal, fruits and vegetables, and lunch meat. Remember that these items will expire, so check the date stamped on the package. These items should be good up to a week after the sell-by date, but after that, your milk will be really thick, and your bread will turn green, so it's best to restock.

By now, your list should be really long—at least the first time you go shopping. There's no way you'll remember to get all those things without it, so bring it with you as we head—

Into the Parking Lot

But which parking lot? Which lucky store is going to add you to its clientele? It may take a few trips to each competitor to see which store fits your personality. That's really how grocery shopping works for food connoisseurs—everyone has a store they like best.

When I went to college, most of the people in my dorm stocked their little refrigerators with stuff from the mini-mart on campus. I thought that the food there was too expensive and they didn't have much of a selection, since it wasn't a large chain. So one day, I took my first solo trip to a real grocery store. That day was the beginning of a four-year relationship between Albertson's and me.

Albertson's advertisements were themed with the phrase, "It's your store." One of their television commercials even showed a grocer delivering medicine to a sick girl so her family wouldn't have to go get it, leaving the girl alone. One night, when my dorm suite was particularly hungry, we decided to call up "our" store and see if they would deliver an ice cream cake to us. They wouldn't. Despite the false advertising, I still made Albertson's my store because it was close to my dorm, it had reasonable prices, and it was clean. That was important, as the sight of maggots in the produce section just doesn't appeal to me. But I had many friends who chose to drive further away and go to the competitor—which did have better prices, but you often had to dodge stacks of empty shipping boxes and Gatorade spills while making your way through the aisles.

Another very smart option when picking your store is to go to a wholesale warehouse-type place, like Sam's Club or Costco. Of course, these places charge an annual membership fee (usually around $40), but if you share a membership with some friends or family members, it is worth it. Although you will find that all the food in these warehouses comes in bulk, you'll probably actually eat sixty packages of Ramen noodles in your first year on your own.

Still, others choose to go to the store that houses their bank's ATM, or the store that is on their way home from work. But, whatever store you choose, make it your store—just don't expect any late night deliveries.

Through the Aisle

You're probably too young to remember this, but there used to be a game show on TV called "Supermarket Sweep," in which two teams of frazzled housewives and the like raced through grocery stores, madly hunting for certain items so they could win blenders, bread makers, or trips to Cancun. Stupid show, I know, but as you get older, your trips to the store will increase, and it will benefit you to know where things are located.

Besides the fact that some stores' aisles are filled with empty boxes and Gatorade spills, most grocery stores are actually very organized to make shopping convenient. And if you're a die-hard list maker, you can even organize your list by the order in which the items can be found in the store to make shopping quicker.

When you enter, grab a cart. It's usually best to start going through the middle aisles, because the side and back walls are filled with cold stuff that you'll probably want to get last to keep it fresh and frozen. Most of the middle aisles will have a sign hanging down from the ceiling telling you what you'll find in that aisle. It will only take you a couple of times asking the clueless fifteen-year-old stock boy where something is before you realize it's faster to read the signs.

The sections are pretty much self-explanatory. The deli has cold cuts. The housewares aisle will contain things like cleaning supplies, batteries, and light bulbs. The dairy section will have milk, eggs, cheese, yogurt, etc. The bread and cereal aisle will have Cheerios, Pop-Tarts, and granola bars—you get the idea. You'll get familiar with what goes where over time.

Some of the larger stores may also have a bank, pharmacy, photo processing lab, and video rental center. Grocery stores are also convenient places to visit an ATM, buy tickets to certain events, and buy stamps. Basically, a trip to a good grocery store can cut your list of errands in half. And once you've swept the aisles, it's time to head . . .

Through the Check-Out Counter

Filling your cart is much more fun than paying for what's in it, but there are a few strategies to lowering your grocery bill.

- **Don't shop on an empty stomach.** Everything will look good, so you'll buy a wider variety of groceries and more of them!

- **Stick to the list.** It's very easy to impulse buy when you're walking through aisles filled with salty snacks; but if you commit to the list, you will most likely stick to the budget.

- **Clip coupons.** Your mailbox and newspapers are chocked full of mailers offering special deals. Look for the coupons—believe me, the savings really add up. Some stores even double coupons, which has allowed me in the past to get items for free. (For example, Glade air freshener: $2.69; my coupon: $1.50 off. At a double coupon store, that equals free air freshener.)

- **Join the club.** Most stores have some special value club for committed shoppers, which may be annoying in that you have to fill out a form and carry your membership card or key chain, but it is definitely worth it to join. These stores offer special prices on many items—but only to members.

- **Don't buy brand names.** Most brand name foods have cheaper cousins labeled "store brand" or "generic." Yes, while RC Cola is not nearly as good as Coca-Cola, people who prefer price to taste won't care. But, taste won't differ too much on generic forms of cereal, mac-n-cheese, and mayonnaise.

- **Check the unit price.** Below each item in the store, there is a tag on the shelf that lists the price. On that tag in really, really small letters, you will see how many cents each ounce of the product costs. So when buying say, cereal, you may instinctually go for the cheaper (smaller) box of Special K, but the larger box is usually the better deal. The stores tell you how much you're paying for each ounce, so use that to determine which product size is actually the best value. Buying in bulk is almost always the best deal!

Out the Door

Time to go home, unload, and eat everything you just bought. Just don't forget to tip the bag boy—if he's cute . . .

chapter 24

Making Sure You're Not the Smelly Kid

How stinky are you?

1. How often do you shower?
    a. When someone tells me to
    b. When my hair starts to look greasy
    c. At least once a day!

2. I keep my deodorant in _____.
    a. A box at the top of my closet—in case I ever need it
    b. In my bathroom drawer
    c. In my back pocket

3. My teeth are flossed _____.
    a. Whenever I visit a dentist
    b. Whenever I get something stuck in them
    c. After every meal

If you scored:

Mostly a's: Putrid!
Mostly b's: Potentially P.U.!
Mostly c's: Pleasant!

Of course you're not the smelly kid! (And you probably really aren't.) But even if you are, you probably don't realize it, because the smelly kid usually isn't smelly *on purpose*. But most kids living at home may need the occasional reminder to change their socks or get a haircut. And in the Real World, the only reminders of your stench will be random acquaintances offering you a stick of gum, a bar of soap, or free use of their shower. Good hygiene can be a challenge, so everyone should get into these hygiene habits, from your head to your toes.

Hair

You don't have to spend $150 a month at the salon to have great hair. In fact, you may be blessed with naturally Pantene-esque golden locks. But if your hair is just kinda "there," follow these hair-boosting tips:

1. **Choose the right shampoo and conditioner.** If your hair is not shiny and silky, it is probably lacking moisture or protein, so choose shampoos with those supplements. If your hair is colored, oily, or dry, choose products whose labels meet your needs. Otherwise, use a balancing formula. It is a good idea to switch brands after finishing a bottle to avoid chemical build up.

2. **Use your products correctly.** Wash your hair as often as it starts to look dirty. For some lucky ones, that may not be every day! When you shampoo, focus on the roots of your hair, where most of the oil lies. When you condition, don't focus on the roots, but on the tips, where most of the damage occurs. Deep condition your hair at least once a week. For styling gels and mousses, use light products that promise the style you are looking for, like "straightening" or "curling."

3. **Don't unnecessarily damage your hair.** Wearing elastic bands excessively, exposing your hair to frequent heat,

and brushing your hair with too much force can damage hair. Also, if you use products to color or highlight your hair, don't overlap the products with every color job, because bleach fries your hair.

4. **Choose the right color and cut.** It's best to leave your hair styling to a professional who listens to what you want, rather than automatically supplying your coif with the latest style. Your hair stylist should be trained enough to recommend a cut that complements both your body and face shape. Hair experts agree that the "golden rule" of great-looking hair color is to go one shade lighter or darker than your natural hue, but of course that rule keeps them in business. For a more subtle enhancement, try highlighting your hair to accentuate your skin tone.

Skincare

The error most people make with their skin care is they either scrub not enough or too much. You should wash your face daily with a mild cleanser suited for your skin type, followed by a moisturizer. When washing your face, gently use your fingers or a soft cloth and always wash in upward, outward strokes. As soon as you get home at night, remove your makeup. If you would like to really pamper your skin, exfoliate weekly and/or apply a face mask for an extra silky, smooth feeling. The most important skincare rule these days is to limit your exposure to the sun, so never go outside without wearing sunscreen with at least a 15 SPF!

Those Pearly Whites

The Academy of General Dentistry conducted a survey that showed that 96 percent of the population thinks a smile is very important to a person's appearance. (That's why your parents sacrificed Europe for your braces.) While visiting the dentist at least twice a year is important for your teeth, a dentist is not your mouth's primary caregiver. You should be a proactive tooth advocate, because dentures are not fun and are very expensive, as your grandparents will tell you. Here are six ways to improve your smile:

1. **"Brush 'em, brush 'em, brush 'em"** is more than just a fun melody from *Grease*. Brush your teeth at least twice a day, and preferably after every meal. Choose an ADA-recommended toothbrush with the right bristle firmness (soft, medium, hard), as recommended by your dentist. Choose a toothpaste with fluoride that doesn't make your teeth feel gritty. If you use a whitening paste, only use it for a week or so at a time, because it can be rough on your enamel. You should spend at least two minutes brushing all three sides of all of your teeth, followed by brushing your tongue, to remove excess bacteria. Ask your dentist to show you the proper way to brush to avoid damaging your gums.

2. **Floss!** It only takes bacteria twenty-four hours to turn into plaque which, if not removed, can cause extensive damage to your teeth and gums. It is essential that you floss thoroughly (yes, even the molars) at least once a day.

3. **Watch your diet.** Sugar is your teeth's enemy; calcium is their friend. Also, avoid foods that stain dishes, because they will also stain your teeth, as will smoking. Frequent snacking and soda-drinking also supply excess phosphoric acid and bacteria that damage your teeth. Follow up your meals and snacks by brushing immediately or by chewing sugarless gum.

4. **Prevent and take care of problems!** Your teeth were not designed to be wrenches, screwdrivers, or scissors. I know from experience that ripping tags with your teeth can result in broken teeth! So, don't use your teeth like they are handymen. On the other hand, if your teeth do chip, break, or cause you any abnormal type of pain, see a dentist immediately.

5. **Drink water.** For sweet breath, the best thing to do is to drink lots of water. Also, regulating your diet with healthy foods and getting enough sleep will affect your breath in a positive way. For the common stink breath everyone endures at one time or another, you can try mouthwash, sprays, parsley, mints and other mouth fresheners. Keep them with you wherever you go. If you have extreme bad breath (halitosis), consult with a doctor for remedies.

6. **Don't forget your smackers!** Your teeth may look great, but no one will look past your lips if they are dry and cracked. Use a lip balm daily with SPF to keep your lips super kissable!

Your Body—and Its Odors

Sadly, you are at the prime age for experiencing body odor. The adolescent years produce hormones that stimulate the growth of your apocrine glands—which increase perspiration. Your sweat is odorless, but when it mixes with the bacteria on your body, it produces a smell. So, the areas of your body that often perspire (underarms) are often the most stinky.

B.O. is an enemy—whether it's your own or someone else's. We have all probably displayed pit stains and inhaled "whew!" moments. If you ever intend on being around people, you may want to regulate your odor. The most obvious ways to smell fresh are to shower often and use deodorant.

How often? If your roommates anonymously leave "Please shower" notes on your door, you may want to turn on the faucet more frequently. You should shower whenever a sniff of your underarms produces a negative result. But you may be immune to your own stench, so for your roommates' sake, bathe (with soap) at least once a day and after any vigorous physical activity!

Washing your body is similar to washing a car. First, rinse off with warm or hot water. Then, work your soap into a rich lather on a washcloth or loofah sponge and scrub your entire body. Follow with another warm rinse. Change your underwear, clothing, and socks daily, and wash them before wearing them again.

When you get out of the shower, use an antiperspirant or deodorant. What's the difference? Deodorant controls odor, while antiperspirant minimizes odor and wetness, so it is more widely used. You may have to reapply throughout the day as needed, so it is a good idea to keep a stick of antiperspirant with you in your car or bag. If you suffer from extreme sweating (hyperhidrosis), consult with a doctor for a prescriptive deodorant powder or stick.

Keep in mind that your diet is your most vital odor factor. Whatever goes into your mouth will eventually come out, either through your skin pores or your—well, your other bodily functions. Avoid junk foods and excessive alcohol, and make sure you keep mealtimes relaxing. Eating fast aids gas production.

If you not only want to avoid smelling bad but also want to smell good, you can roll around in a flower bed every day—or try applying perfume or cologne. Pick a scent that fits your personality, and spray it on your pulse points, located on your neck, wrists, and behind your knees. Just don't go overboard—if your "Curve" or "Pleasures" is detected more than three feet away, decrease your dosage by merely spraying a squirt in front of you, then walking into the mist.

"Down There"

Uh, not a topic for dinnertime conversation. But, just a quick word about pelvic-area odors—geared toward the ladies. During your menstrual cycles, change your tampons or pads frequently (at least once every 4–8 hours). Wash thoroughly with a mild soap, but be sure to rinse well to avoid infection or irritation. Although "douches" were invented to eliminate odors, they are not all medically safe, so check with a doctor before using them.

Now, that wasn't so bad. Even those pleasantly smelling people may have learned something new. If only all of the world would heed this advice!

part

Surviving the Social Scene

chapter 25

How much fun are you on vacation?

1. Your last spring break was spent _____.
    a. At MTV's Panama City beach party!
    b. At Grandma's house in Oklahoma
    c. In my bed

2. Spontaneity makes for _____.
    a. Fun trips
    b. Chaotic trips
    c. Disastrous trips

3. Your vacation luck is best described by the movie:
    a. *National Lampoon's Vegas Vacation*
    b. *Dude! Where's My Car?*
    c. *Titanic*

If you scored:

Mostly a's: You're on the postcard.
Mostly b's: You send boring postcards.
Mostly c's: I'll send you a postcard.

The classic road trip is spontaneously planned and carried out in the same night. Five or more wired young people cram into a car with a box of Twinkies and the entire Jimmy Buffet collection, and drive to Vegas—or some other God-forsaken place with cheap hotel rooms and something slightly illegal to do. While these trips always create the best memories (don't forget your camera), most road trips are planned somewhat in advance with a bit more organization.

If you are a planner, there are four aspects to consider when detailing your voyage: travel companions, destination, mode of transportation, and travel gear.

Traveling Companions

Choose your car buddies carefully. A well-rounded road trip partner is adventurous, spontaneous, and flexible. He brings his own money and clothes and has a few long-lost pals along the way whose homes (or the like) you can crash at, if need be. He'll listen to your music, and share some of his own tunes, but won't sing along too loudly, unless the song requires passenger backup. You should be able to enjoy comfortable silence with this person, but he should also know the lyrics to "99 Bottles of Beer on the Wall."

A good traveling friend doesn't mind going off and exploring your destination on his own, and allows you to do the same, but will always accompany you for your nights out on the town. Try to pick someone who is in the same income bracket as you are, because a Hilton heiress may have a different idea of what makes a hotel suitable than someone who considers Motel 6 a luxury resort. And just in case you didn't know, a road trip is the best way to determine whether or not you're compatible with a member of the opposite sex. If you can together endure fourteen hours of desert driving with a broken air conditioner, consider yourselves a match made in heaven.

Destination

So, where are you going to go? Pretty much every state offers a campground, river, beach, or amusement park worth traveling to. There are even fun road trip destinations in Nebraska—Sarpy County boasts the nation's largest parade. (Now, that's a wild ride.) Other fun, but more extravagant trips are all-inclusive cruises and destinations like Club Med or Sandals, health spas, and resorts. Check with a travel agent, AAA, or *www.randmcnally.com* for help planning the perfect destination, tailored to your budget and personality. Those sources can also provide you with information about your road trip's weather and traffic conditions, as well as lodging accommodations, restaurants, and events once you get there.

If you're looking for a fun trip tailored to your personality, pick your vacation mood and one of these classic vacation locations:

Young at Heart
Disneyland
Orlando's Magic Kingdom
Six Flags
Sea World

History Buffs
Washington, DC
Boston, MA
Philadelphia, PA
San Francisco, CA

Nature Lovers
Zion's National Park
Hike the Rockies
Whitewater rafting
Yellowstone
Lake Tahoe

Meditators
Hilton Head
Atlantic lighthouses
Pacific coast beaches
Colorado's mountains
Jackson Hole, WY

Partiers
Florida's beaches
Las Vegas
College towns
New Orleans Mardi Gras

Sight-Seers
New York City
Mount Rushmore
Grand Canyon
LA/Hollywood

Even if your destination's best features are rained out or closed for the season, remember that during a road trip, most of your fun lies in the journey, anyway!

Mode of Transportation

Yes, smarty pants, "road trip" means to drive on the road, but people travel these days by planes, trains, or automobiles. Whatever mode you choose, remember the following travel tips.

Cars

Though a slightly lengthy way to travel, you can never beat the fun you'll have in a car. The more passengers you invite, the more gas money and extra drivers you'll get (as well as backseat drivers). Have your automobile checked out by a mechanic before you leave, and make sure to keep your gas tank at least one-quarter full your entire trip. Despite its historical significance, you don't want to be stranded on Route 66 with an empty tank. Also, check your oil and wiper fluid levels often at rest stops—because those things come in handy on the road.

Try to conquer most of your traveling ground in the daylight or when you are most alert, and make sure you have at least one other passenger, music, books on tape, and snacks help keep you awake along the way. Also, make sure you have a roadside assistance kit that includes the following: jumper cables, water bottle, spare tire kit, flashlight with batteries, flares, anti-nausea pills, blankets, and a cell phone.

Bored in the car and traveling with a large group? Try these car games:

- **"License Plate"**—A road trip classic. Get out a sheet of paper and a pen, and write down the name of each state once, as you see it on the license plate of a passing car. Set up a reward like, "After twenty-five states, we stop at Dairy Queen!"

- **"Alphabet Signs"**—Assign everyone a less common letter of the alphabet, like j, q, v, x, and z. Every time a person sees his letter on a sign, he gets a point. Whoever has the most points after one hour (if you can play that long) wins.

- **"Scavenger Hunt"**—Before you begin playing, make a list of items to find on the road like black-and-white cows, haystacks, windmills, and hitchhikers. Cross them off as you see them.

- **"20 Questions"**—Another car classic. Have someone pick a word that is either a person, place, or thing (or make up your own). The other players try to guess the item by asking fewer than twenty questions that can be answered with "yes" or "no." (Hint: Choosing the word "napkin" has a 5-0 success record in my car.)

- **"I'm going on a road trip and I'm bringing"**—Go around in a circle and have each person repeat that phrase and fill in the blank with something that starts with each letter of the alphabet, in order. When it's the next person's turn, she must repeat all the things said before in order, then add one of her own, or she's out.

Planes

The most convenient way to travel, flying gets you there fast, and sometimes for cheaper than your auto fuel bill would be. But, it eliminates the possibility of seeing the world's largest haystack along the way. If you are flying, make sure you arrive at the airport well in advance (check the airport's recommendations), and make sure you bring the required identification (license, passport, visa). Don't bring anything that will be taken by security, because you won't get your sewing scissors back. When you are booking your ticket or if you check in early enough, you may be able to request an aisle, window, or exit row seat for more room. And if you want to speed up the airport process by not having to wait at the baggage claim area, try to take all of your luggage as carry-ons.

If you are trying to lower your air fare, fly at a time and day of the week that is less busy, and always stay over on a Saturday night. Also, if you get a flight on a charter plane, or one with more than two legs in your trip, you can lower your fare. There are several websites, like *www.cheaptickets. com, www.travelocity.com,* and *www.priceline.com* that can get you discount fares. If you are not in a hurry and don't mind the price of airport food, you may be asked to volunteer your seat if the airline has overbooked your flight. In return, they'll give you airfare vouchers that will be well worth your time waiting for the next flight.

Buses and Trains

If you really want to see the country and meet some interesting people, call Amtrak or Greyhound. Buses and trains are definitely the most affordable traveling options, but they give a whole new meaning to the phrase "road trip." (If you don't believe me, may you enjoy your extra-long journey with sailors, Tibetan monks, and aspiring country singers.)

Time to Pack!

Ah, I can already smell the salty breeze! Now, keep that in mind when you are packing. A salty breeze requires a beach towel, sunglasses, bathing suit, sunscreen, and a best-seller. A ski trip requires snow clothes, a hat, sunglasses, sunscreen, and a swimsuit for hot tubbing. Make a list a week before your vacation of what exactly you will need to bring, tailored to the place you are going, and your activities once you get there. Don't forget your athletic equipment, pajamas, sleeping gear—if you are on the floor—and a nice outfit in case you go out on the town. And always bring the following: vital identification information, traveler's checks, cash for tipping, camera and film, photocopies of your license, passport and important phone numbers in case you're robbed or stranded somewhere, and your insurance cards. Pack all of your things in durable, labeled bags that are easy to carry.

On vacations you are supposed to "vacate" your normal, crazy life, so don't overbook your free time. Just kick back and relax. And on your road trip, even if the engine of your car falls out, you're stranded in Oklahoma City for a week, then you're forced to drive through a hailstorm with your windows down because of the fumes from the fuel that the mechanics spilled into your car's upholstery while they were replacing your engine, just remember: road trips are great training for the toils of the Real World.

chapter 26

The "It" Factor:
Four Steps to Small-Town Fame

How "with it" are you?

1. Could you go to a movie by yourself?
   a. That pretty much describes my Friday nights
   b. No way! What if someone saw me? I'd be mortified!
   c. Sure, why not? If no one else wanted to see the movie I did

2. Could you roll out of bed, throw on a hat, and meet your friends for brunch?
   a. What's "brunch?"
   b. Of course—after a quick stop at the salon
   c. Yeah—I got that natural thing going on

3. What phrase best describes your social group?
   a. Lazy punks
   b. I only associate with the popular crowd
   c. I have friends everywhere—from all groups and all walks of life

---

If you scored:

Mostly a's: Not quite "with it."
Mostly b's: Snob? Yes. "It?" No.
Mostly c's: Definitely "it!"

Are you the lifeblood of your social group? Could you have replaced Marilyn Monroe in *How to Be Beverly Hills Popular*? Did Dale Carnegie observe you for inspiration when he wrote *How To Win Friends and Influence People*? Were you well liked in high school, and even more so now? Do you have a coolness about you that is more magnetic than a refrigerator? Are you an Angelina, a Blake, a Brad, or a Tom? Are you "It?"

Chances are—probably not . . . yet. Few people ever achieve "it"-ness. It seems like an art form that would take years to conquer, but it's really not that hard. The "it" factor is not something automatically assigned to the "in crowd." In fact, many of the typically popular kids in high school are very much *not* it, because they are so concerned with trying to show everyone how cool they are. Truly "it" people are down to earth, and although sometimes aloof, they are actually very nice to everyone. They don't follow trends; they start them. People are more excited to go to parties knowing a certain "it" person may be there; and the party doesn't get started until she arrives.

"It" people ooze confidence and respect. They fight for what they believe in. They know it is better to be respected than liked. They are not afraid to go places alone, because they are comfortable with themselves. They don't talk about other people; they talk about ideas. They have style, but it is more about who they are than how they look. Everybody likes "it" people—or at least admires their position. "It" people are naturally cool, but they don't care if they are, which makes them even more so. "It" people unintentionally break hearts, are unknowingly surrounded by a fan club, and undeniably succeed in whatever they do—just because they do it their way.

Following are the four qualities that characterize the "it" factor. Although you may have to work hard to achieve complete "it"-ness, initiating any of these qualities into your personality will only give you more dates, more friends, and more success in life.

1 **Love yourself!** But keep it to yourself. The "it" factor's primary component is confidence. So what if one of your legs is longer than the other? Who cares? Common problem with many people. So you can't afford to buy this season's wardrobe? So what! By next season, it will be out of style anyway. So you have a loud, shrieking laugh that turns heads? So does Julia Roberts. Love your looks, your quirky sense of humor, your clothes, your laugh, your skin color—it's you. It's perfect! No one could pull it off better.

Radiate confidence, but not cockiness. Know that you are okay, but don't feel the need to tell everyone else how great you are. You don't need to toss your hair and wear micro-mini skirts to look hot. If you're beautiful, people will notice that without your epidermal advertisement (and you'll leave more to the imagination). If you achieve an incredible accomplishment, you don't have to tell everyone. Awards are given at public ceremonies that will probably be broadcast by the news anyway. Be modest about your achievements, and people will just be more intrigued by you.

When I was in college, there was a guy in one of my humanities classes who was absolutely *gorgeous!* That alone made me want to get to know him better, but he turned out to be pretty cool, too. After talking to him for an entire semester and still not knowing much about him, I asked around and found out he had modeled with a very prestigious agency, he was brilliant, and his dad was a billionaire. Because I found out those things from someone else, it made the guy all the more appealing.

2 **Dare.** The reason that some people are so much fun is because the "it" factor does not allow for inhibitions. "It" people are daredevils, risk takers, and initiators. They jump onstage at Amateur Night, volunteer to be the hypnotist's bait, and try out for reality TV shows. Skinny dipping? Sure.

Bungee jumping? Why not. "It" people have learned that life is supposed to be lived. Ferris Bueller was a classic in this category. (By the way, that movie is the perfect training video for mastering the "it" factor). When Ferris wants to impress his girlfriend, he "borrows" the Ferrari of his friend's dad, weasels his way into a snooty restaurant, and jumps onto the main float at a huge parade and serenades her without any qualms.

"It" people never say phrases like, "I don't know. What do you want to do?" "It" people are more likely to call you up at 3 a.m. and say, "Come on, let's go hot tubbing!" "It" people set the plans, invite fun people, and can even make playing pinochle at a convalescent home a thrilling adventure. "It" people think big and live big. They own disco balls—and frequently use them. They have been overseas—on a whim. They have dream jobs, because they aren't afraid to go for it. "It" people knock down walls and step over barriers. All because they dare.

3 **Be interested in others.** Consider the quote: "If everyone were a star, who would listen and clap?" While you may be a star among your peers, without their clapping, you wouldn't shine so brightly. So, return the favor. Take a genuine interest in others. Remember names. Look people in the eye. Ask questions. And most important, listen to their answers. Avoid the classic technique of an annoying conversationalist who listens to someone's story of success or failure and then immediately turns the focus back on himself. That completely discredits any sign of genuine friendship. Instead, be sincerely happy for others' successes.

I had a friend in high school whose mother was famous for her competitive desire to top everyone else's stories. It became quite comical, in fact, especially after a bunch of friends and our families had traveled to Texas to attend a Cotton Bowl football game one winter. My dad was a former college football player, and he scored my family fifty-yard line, front row seats, right behind the players. The entire game, we had a perfect view of the game and talked to the team; and afterwards, one of the players took my little brother onto the field and gave him his sweat bands and a Cotton Bowl teddy bear. After the game, we met up with my friend's mother, and once she found out where we had sat, she seriously exclaimed, "Oh, I feel so bad for you, you should have been sitting by us. We were right behind the band in the end zone, and nothing can beat the enthusiasm you feel when you sit behind the band!" Don't be like that.

On the other hand, nothing is more impressive than someone—and especially someone bearing the "it" factor—who remembers facts about a person. I once competed in a scholarship pageant for teenagers where I met the country singing group Diamond Rio. They were very nice and offered me backstage passes to the next concert they would be performing in near my town. I attended one year later, and when I walked backstage, the lead singer loudly exclaimed, "It's Miss Tennessee! Autumn, how are ya?" While they made me feel pretty important, it just showed how very much "it" *they* were.

4 **Be interesting.** Do you watch the news, or do you watch soap operas? Do you read books, or do you read fashion magazines? Do you vote, or do you just complain about our political system? Are you constantly trying to improve, or do you just think you're perfect and everyone else isn't? "It" people are interesting because they know and care about a variety of subjects. Intelligence is very appealing to others, and I'm not just talking about book smarts. "It" people don't spend all their time at social events—although they probably could. They have hobbies and interests, they take classes, they volunteer, they run marathons. They are always doing something. "It" people have ideas and make them happen. They don't have time to sit around and gossip about who's wearing what to the Oscars; they are planning their own

Oscar party, or designing their own outfit. They have lives. And they live them!

chapter 27

Dating Do's and Don'ts

What kind of a date are you?

1. How far in advance should you ask someone out?
    a. About a week
    b. A day
    c. What? I just show up!

2. A typical date for you is:
    a. Dinner and a movie
    b. A sushi bar and a comedy club
    c. Chillin' in my van

3. Who pays?
    a. The guy, of course
    b. Whoever asks
    c. My parents

If you scored:
Mostly a's: Cotillion graduate
Mostly b's: Contemporary catnip
Mostly c's: Courtesy date

Horror Date #1: You go out with someone a little "different" because—well, you just plain feel sorry for him, and the entire date (as well as four phone calls the next day) consist of him asking you over and over again why girls don't like him, and then finally, why you don't like him.

Horror Date #2: You go out with another "nice guy" who insists that you pray in the car for your date's welfare—which actually isn't a bad idea—after you spend the entire night being forced to hold his clammy hand while ice skating (i.e., you dragging him along the ground) and checking out the two really hot hockey players at the rink, hoping they think your date is a socially challenged cousin. Luckily, he has you home by ten.

Horror Date #3: You swear off dating any more "different" or "nice" guys and dare to ask the love of your freshman-year life, a real "bad boy," to the Sadie Hawkins dance—and he says "yes!" Only, you find out last minute that he is court-ordered homebound for vandalizing his neighbor's backyard. But he has arranged for you to go with his "really cool" friend, who turns out to look like Jared the Subway Miracle Diet guy in his "before" pictures, and acts as exciting as a veggie on wheat.

Is your dating luck anything like mine? Don't despair— the average single person goes out on one good date for every 467 bad ones. Yet, we still do it. For centuries, naïve daters just like you and me have endured being stood up, left at parties while your date is making out with your roommate, and set up on countless blind dates during which you wish you really were blind.

Sometimes, the 1950's diner and drive-in dates don't sound so bad, because at least then they knew what to expect. These days, with dating game shows, services, psychics, coffee house dates and online matchmaking, trying to find your soul mate is as complicated as trying to get through airport security while wearing an underwire bra. While dating traditions have revolutionized over the last fifty years, some truths still hold in the dating world: shower, don't chew with your mouth open, and don't kiss and tell the entire locker room. But if you are looking to find true love in this world (and who isn't?), you may want to pay attention to these time-tested do's and don'ts.

Getting the Date

Do:

- Take risks! Ask out your crush—she'll probably be flattered. And these days, girls are allowed to ask guys out, too.

- Ask in advance—but not too far, or you'll appear desperate.

- Be confident. Mentally condition yourself to think that the person you ask out is lucky to be seen with you. If she says no, her loss!

- Act interested in the person. Don't make him think you're being dared or bribed to ask him out.

- Play a little hard-to-get. Sounding too available will make you seem like you never have dates, plans, or friends.

- When asking someone out, have a plan in mind and make it sound fun. Something like, "Hey, a bunch of people are going bowling Friday night—I was wondering if you'd want to come along—my treat," works better than, "Hey, are you free Friday night? Do you want to maybe hang out or do something or whatever?"

- When you first go out with someone new, go with a group so there isn't as much pressure, and so you get to see how your date interacts with your friends.

Don't:

- Act desperate or try to make someone feel sorry for you.

- Be rude to someone who asks you out, even if you are not interested. Just politely say no.

- Go out alone with someone who you don't know very well.

- Use lame, stale, or cheesy pick-up lines. If you insist on using pickup lines, use humor and flattery to lighten the moment. And if you are a frequent pick-up liner and you are tired of telling people they look like angels who dropped from heaven, you need a quarter to call home, or her legs must be tired because she's been running through your mind all night, consider some of these overheard come-ons that may still be original in your neck of the woods.

> *Warning: The following may produce gagging.*
> *Use caution if you have a weak stomach or*
> *strong aversion to creepy guys.*

- "Did we go to a different school together?"

- "I'm new in town. Can you give me directions to your apartment?"

- "Were you talking to me?" (No.) "Well, then, please start."

- "Do you know what would look good on you? Me."

- "Are we related? Do you want to be?"

- "If you were a booger, I'd pick you first."

- "Excuse me, I think I've dropped something. My JAW!"

- "If I followed you home, would you keep me?"

- "Wouldn't we look cute on the top of a wedding cake together?"

- "If you were words on a page, you'd be what they call 'Fine Print.'"

- "Hey! You were great on *Baywatch* last night!"

- "I lost my phone number; can I borrow yours?"

- "Hi, I'm writing a term paper on the finer things in life. Can I interview you?"

- "You're so fine you make me stutter. Wh-wh-what's your name?"

- "See my friend over there? He wants to know if you think I'm cute."

- "Is it hot in here, or is it just you?"

- "Inheriting $60 million doesn't mean much if you don't have anyone to share it with."

- "Can I buy you a drink? Or do you just want the money?"

- "Hi! Are you cute?"

- "Hi. I make more money than you could ever spend. Wanna go out?"

- "Baby, I'm like American Express. You shouldn't go anywhere without me."

- "Is your name Beverly? Cause you've got some nice, expensive hills."

- "I want you to have my children. In fact, you can have them right now; they're out in my car."

- "I may not be the best looking guy here, but I'm the only one talking to you."

And if you are so lucky as to receive any of the following classic pick-up lines from a real weirdo, try these rebuttals:

- "Have we met?" "Yes, I'm the receptionist at the V.D. clinic."

- "Is this seat empty?" "Yes, and this one will be, too, if you sit down."

- "Have I seen you somewhere before?" "Yes, that's why I don't go there anymore."

- "So, what do you do for a living?" "I'm a female impersonator."

- "Do I know you?" "No, and let's keep it that way."

On the Date

Do:

- Be somewhat on time.

- Be nice to your date's roommates or family. They can be a useful fan club later.

- Complement your date on something, even if it's his shoes.

- Try to have fun—even if you don't like the person. There's no point in totally wasting your night.

- Keep your romantic feelings to yourself, until the time is right. The first date is not the right time to tell your date you hope your children look like her.

- Mind your manners: don't burp, eat rudely, or pass any form of gas. If you're a guy, be a gentleman—most girls still love guys who open doors!

- Ask your date questions and listen to his answers. Give him a chance!

- If you asked the person out, have enough money to pay. Doing dishes at a five-star restaurant isn't a great end to a first date.

- Be creative; do something different! Cook together, take a dance class, make pottery, go bowling, picnic on a roof, do karaoke, go skiing, go to an art exhibit or a museum, play hide-and-seek at the grocery store. Make whatever you do fun and memorable.

- Dress appropriately and remember your hygiene: after you shower, brush your teeth and apply deodorant. Bring mints/gum for post-meal close-ups.

- Walk the person to the door at the end of the date. Say thank-you.

Don't:

- Honk. Always go to the door!

- Be really late (unreliable) or really early (eager).

- Ignore or act rudely toward your date's friends & family.

- Complement everything about your date. Save some for later.

- Act bored. Only boring people get bored.

- Hit on other people! (Even if you don't like your date.)

- Go back "to my place" on a first date; in fact, don't even kiss on the first date, because then (if you're interested in the person), you give him a good reason to go out with you again. Keep him guessing.

- Kiss the person if you don't like her, and then complain, "I don't know why she keeps calling."

- Ask stupid questions like, "Do you like me?" "Do you

think I have a chance?" "Do you believe in love at first date?" Be cool.

After the Date

Do:

- Say thank you at the door. If you two are both interested, call within the next day or two and set up another rendezvous.

- If you're not interested, tell the person in a polite way. Use the classics, "I think we're better off as friends" or "I don't see us having a romantic future," instead of lines that can get you in trouble like, "I've joined a cult that doesn't allow any contact with the opposite sex," or "I'm moving to Barbados."

- If the person didn't make you gag, give him a chance. Accept another date with an open mind.

Don't:

- Call the next morning and say you're in love.

- Lie. If you're not interested and she is, tell her.

If You're "Dating"

Do:

- Do a variety of activities together to really get to know the person. Most people are fun in a movie theatre, but not everyone likes roller coasters.

- Get to know the person's friends, and make sure you get along with them.

- Make sure the person knows what's most important to you: your values, interests, hobbies, goals, etc.

Don't:

- Take things too fast. It will be harder to back out later.

- Cheat (unless you're looking for a quick out of your relationship).

- Absolutely don't put up with any form of abuse.

If You're "Serious"

Do:

- Get to know the person's family. Make sure you can get along with them well enough to endure family dinners.

- Make sure you are on the same page—or at least in agreement that it's okay to be different—with important topics like religion, politics, family planning, and finances.

- Find out the person's sexual history (for your own protection from disease).

- Know the difference between infatuation and true love. Would you still love this person if you were blind or he were paraplegic?

- Get premarital counseling, if you're considering that route. Even solid couples can benefit from counseling, as it reaffirms that they have discussed all of the important issues before taking the big step.

Don't:

- Feel pressured to make any commitment you're not ready for. A person who truly loves you will let you take your time in deciding when you're ready for a major life-changing moment like marriage.

- Forget that a long-lasting relationship is based on much

more than physical attraction and sexual compatibility. Make sure your relationship benefits from these traits as well: mutual support, affection, companionship, friendship, devotion, loyalty, respect, patience, forgiveness, and admiration.

Despite dating horror stories, long-lost loves, and broken hearts, love still exists and it is worth it. If you haven't already, one day you may meet someone who you will call "your better half," who completes your sentences, whose kisses make you weak in the knees, and who you can sit in silence with and feel more comfortable than if you were alone. You will share tears over the birth of your little miracle, believe your fixer-upper is paradise, and dream of the day when you'll both sit on your porch, wrinkled and hunched over, but smiling as the sun sets behind an apple tree you planted together sixty years ago. Someday, you can meet the love of your life. I know, because I have.

chapter 28

It's My Party, I Can Cry if I Want to:
How to Host a Party Without Too Many Tears

How fun are you at a party?

1. Where can you be found at a party?
    a. Center stage
    b. On a crowded couch
    c. With a lampshade over my head

2. Your favorite party song:
    a. *Get This Party Started!*
    b. *Hokey Pokey*
    c. *Every Party Needs a Pooper, That's Why We Invited You*

3. "R.S.V.P." means:
    a. Respond s'il vous plait.
    b. Show up—if you can.
    c. Bring a friend—or a few!

If you scored:
Mostly a's: I am the party!
Mostly b's: I am as fun as the food is good.
Mostly c's: I wasn't invited.

Remember all those "my parents are out of town so come over tonight" parties in high school? Well now, you big kid you, the Real World says you get to have them whenever you want! But the beer bashes will get old, and you'll start to realize what your parents meant by "that gunk your friends left in the carpet" after a few come-on-overs that result in carpet cleaning. When you enter the Real World, you need to know how to throw a real party—the kind that will spark people to say, "Hey, are you having your party this year?"

No matter how formal they are, memorable parties project a mood, based on their theme or purpose. The theme should first be apparent with the party invitations, and then carried through with the party's location, decorations, music, food, and entertainment. If you take the time beforehand to plan out each of these aspects, your party will flow together, and your guests will deem you Party Master. So, pay attention to the details.

Theme/Purpose

Why take the time to clean your place before and after your guests come over if you aren't celebrating an occasion? Your party's theme may be a given—it might be your best friend's birthday, the Fourth of July, or you might be in the position to host a bridal or baby shower. Or you may just want to have a party. To spice it up, make up a theme like a Mexican Fiesta, Back to School Bash, or Summer Luau. Your theme will give you guidance for the rest of the details.

Budget

After you've picked your theme, it's time to consider the not-so-fun stuff—the budget. Parties have a crazy way of getting out of hand; and if you don't plan ahead, you may find yourself spending two, five, or ten times more than you planned on your next bash. So first, sit down with a pen and paper and write down how much you have to spend. Maybe a friend (or two) is willing to chip in on the party with you. Or even better, maybe your great-aunt's second cousin twice removed is more than happy to fund the entire bridal shower for your great-aunt's sixth wedding this fall. Wahoo! Go to town. But still, you will need to consider all of the following costs in your budget, and stick to it! Or else you'll be charging entrance fees to your party guests.

Invitations

First, consider how many people you want to invite. That will determine how much money you plan on spending. If your party is informal, like the classic living room college parties, your invitations will probably be informal fliers, posted signs, or word-of-mouth invites. But if your party is more formal, you will want to make or purchase invitations that go with your theme and mail them out at least two weeks in advance so people have time to RSVP—which does mean to "respond please" as to whether or not they will be attending.

On your invitations, announce the theme of the party and clarify the who, what, when and where. Do you want only your invitees to come, or do you mind if they bring guests? You need to specify that on the invitation, as well as if you want the person to bring anything, like if you were hosting a pot luck dinner. Include directions if most people don't know where the location is, and include an RSVP number if you need to know the approximate count of guests. And if your party guests should wear certain attire, designate that as well.

Location

If the party will be at your place, all you'll need to do is clean up and set up. But if you are planning on reserving a social hall, banquet room, restaurant, or other location, your preparations will need to be taken care of far in advance. Make sure you reserve the location through the proper channels, and have them commit to leaving the place in good condition. Many party halls will allow you to also use their tables and chairs. You will probably have to pay a security deposit in case any of your guests gets a little too wild, and yes you—not your guests—will be responsible for any damages!

Decorations

Your decorations can be as simple as turning the lights off and turning on a disco ball, or as complex as hanging crepe streamers, renting garland trellises, lighting candles, and buying floral arrangements or balloons. At a formal party, you will probably want to arrange nice table settings before the guests arrive. Remember the décor of your party place sets the atmosphere of the entire event—whether you just set up some chairs on your back patio or hang a thousand glittery stars in a banquet hall.

Food

Ah—the heart of the party! If you serve good food and drinks, people will stay. The best way to handle the food at a big party is to arrange to pick up take-out from a restaurant or to hire a caterer, because you will be busy enough with the other details. But if you do make the food yourself, just make sure everything is prepared well ahead of time so that your guests won't be impatient and hungry, but late enough that it is the right temperature. Also, make sure your food sticks with the theme, because corn dogs just don't set the right mood at a wedding reception. And remember that a nice presentation can make something that only tastes okay seem like it tastes wonderful.

Most party hosts opt for buffet-style presentation, at

which guests can pick and choose their own chips and dip as they like. For very formal occasions, you may want to consider a formal sit-down dinner or hire servers to walk around with trays, as is common at cocktail parties. If you have a formal dinner, you should arrange place cards beforehand, with guests sitting next to people with whom you think they would be most compatible. In case you didn't attend an etiquette class, here is how you set a formal place setting. (If you are not serving soup, dessert, rolls, or more than one beverage, simply remove the extra dishes and utensils.)

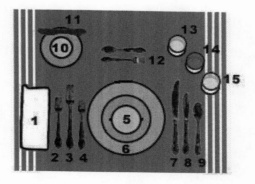

1. Napkin
2. Salad fork
3. Appetizer/fish fork
4. Dinner fork
5. Soup bowl and plate
6. Dinner plate
7. Dinner knife
8. Appetizer/fish knife
9. Soup spoon
10. Bread and butter plate
11. Butter knife
12. Dessert utensils
13. Water goblet
14. Red wine goblet
15. White wine goblet

It is always better to have too much food than not enough! So, stock those trays and keep the drinks flowing—and your guests should stick around.

286 • Real World 101

Music/Entertainment

Unless your party is centered around another form of entertainment, you should always have music playing. The easiest option is to simply turn on your sound system with music that is right for the mood. But if you want to get people on their feet and dancing, hire a band or deem one of your buddies DJ for the evening. If you are having a formal party, stick to classical tunes—you know, the ones your parents have programmed into their car's speed set buttons.

If you really want to add some fun to your party, consider hiring outside entertainment. You can book dancers (and no, I am not suggesting the stripping kind), comedians, magicians, caricaturists, or anyone else with an unusual hobby, like balloon art or pantomime. Just avoid clowns—many people fear them. Hiring a photographer also gives guests something fun to do, and it provides them a keepsake for the party as well. Word to the wise: Don't expect your guests to pay for their entertainment. You're footing the bill for this one, babe.

Playing Host

If you are hosting your own party, then you will probably not have the opportunity to enjoy it as much as everyone else. Instead you'll be busy greeting guests, taking coats and making sure everyone is having fun. It is your duty to keep the food and drinks stocked, to keep the noise level low enough to avoid police visits, and to make sure nothing gets broken. And after, you get the fun job of cleaning everything up! Be gracious toward your guests, though, because you really should be flattered that they took the time to show up!

Party in a Paragraph

So, you're willing to put in the work, but need help coming up with a theme? Here is what an event planner would charge hundreds of dollars to tell you. While these party ideas may seem quite elaborate, you can pick and choose the features you want to spend the time and money on.

Oscar Party

If you and at least five of your friends watch this annual four-hour event, consider making it more fun by playing right along! My grandma's annual Oscar is a much anticipated family event, but this party can work for any other awards show as well:

Invitations: Make them formal and fun, in gold-lined envelopes with the Oscar emblem copied and pasted from the website. Tell your guests to "dress for the Oscars." After all, half of the event is what people wear!

Location/Decorations: A home with a big screen is the best place for this soiree. Decorations can be simple; you can make some fake Oscar trophies or buy them in Los Angeles gift shops next time you head out west, or you can find them online. Ask movie theaters for movie posters and display them, as well as copies or pictures of the movies or stars who are up for awards.

Food: Display hors d'oeuvres and dessert, or serve food that correlates with the movie themes.

Entertainment: When everyone arrives, have them fill out ballot sheets with their guesses as to who will win each award. Arrange prizes for the guest with the most correct answers, and for the guests who pick the winners of the big categories. Then, of course watch the Oscars!

Survivor/Bachelor/Biggest Loser Party

Do you have a favorite TV show and a crew of fellow groupies? Throw a party based on the show's season premier or finale. Here is what we did for a Survivor party:

Invitations: Write the party details on leaves in a black marker, and deliver them to the guests. Tell them to dress in their best island attire or as their favorite character.

Location/Decorations: Have this party at a house in front of a TV. For the Survivor motif, display tiki torches or candles and camping gear.

Food: Serve rice, and have guests auction for additives to their meal (like beans, chicken, vegetables, and dressing) with fake money they earn from completing a Survivor trivia questionnaire.

Entertainment: Watch the show! Afterwards, make up some "challenges" of your own for immunity from having to help clean up!

Luau

Luaus are a great way to celebrate the summer, or any occasion in warm climates. Their mood is light, festive, and casual.

Invitations: Buy cheap flower leis for everyone, and with string, dangle from them separate cards that announce each detail of the party. Ask everyone to wear Hawaiian or beach attire.

Location/Decorations: An outdoor setting is a must, and a beachy, tropical atmosphere is preferable. Use tiki torches or lanterns for light, and decorate with any beach or pool supplies. Greet your guests with real flower leis.

Food: A slow-roasted pig over an open fire is a luau tradition (and makes for a very authentic decoration). But if that grosses you out, serve pork or barbecue, salads, rolls, and don't forget the poi.

Music/Entertainment: Play tropical music throughout the whole party, and have a Limbo competition. Consider hiring Polynesian or fire dancers to perform for real entertainment. A luau should be filled with music and dancing.

Harvest/Halloween Hoedown

For an extra twist to a fall party, go down home and have a hoedown!

Invitations: Buy several miniature pumpkins (they're cheap) and write the party details on them in a black, permanent marker; or cut out pumpkins or ghosts from construction paper, and write the information on those. If you're focusing on Halloween, guests should wear costumes. Otherwise, tell them to dress Western.

Location/Decorations: An old barn makes for the perfect location for this party; but if that isn't possible, your house, a field, or any large gathering area will do. Decorate with scarecrows, lit jack-o-lanterns, and harvest cornucopias. Throw around some haystacks and pitchforks, and don't forget to add the Halloween elements: ghosts, cobwebs, witches' hats, and steaming (dry ice) cauldrons.

Food: If you are planning on serving dinner, make a Chuck wagon-type meal—with beef or chicken, potatoes, vegetables, rolls, and Dutch oven cobbler. For an easier fall meal, serve chili and cornbread. Good snacks to serve are caramel apples, oatmeal cookies, and popcorn.

Music/Entertainment: Background music should be Halloween-based or country-western. You have a lot of entertainment options here. Rent a wagon and take guests on hayrides, or create a miniature haunted house in your garage. Guests can bob for apples and enter a costume contest. Or, hire a line dance teacher to get everyone do-si-doing.

Murder Mystery Dinner

This is a role-playing board game you can buy in the game section of many stores. The game instructions will suggest the theme, decorations and food you should serve. All invitees must commit to come, and dress and act according to their character as you play the "game," which is to decide which of you committed a murder, based on the provided clues. The game lasts about four hours and is a very fun way to unveil the creative, mysterious side of your friends.

Bridal Shower

Girls, when your best friend or roommate gets married, it is usually your responsibility to host a shower beforehand. Showers can be coed, but most guys will thank you if you leave them off the invite list. Generally, showers last about two hours, although they can be "open house" style, at which guests come and go as they please. Indicate as such on your invitation.

Invitations: It is customary to ask the bride for a guest list, and to send each person on the list an invitation two to three weeks in advance (or further in advance if they will be traveling long distances). The purpose of a shower is to "shower" the bride with gifts, and you can try to make the gifts relate to a theme. If a bride will be having many showers, you can designate yours to a particular room in the house like a "Kitchen Shower" (cooking supplies) or a "Bedroom Shower" (i.e., lingerie from the bride's close friends; pillowcases and candles from her older relatives). Or you can throw an "A to Z" shower, and assign everyone to bring a gift that begins with a certain letter; or a "Months of the Year" shower, with everyone choosing a gift that relates to a particular time of year. Many brides register for gifts they would like at particular stores, and it is not inappropriate to let guests know of this, if they ask.

Location/Decorations: Someone's home is the most comfortable atmosphere for a shower. But, if you don't think you'll have enough room at your house, consider renting a room in a restaurant. For decorations, use linens and balloons in the bride's wedding colors, and display a picture of the bride and groom-to-be.

Food: Finger foods are customary at showers, unless you hold the shower during a mealtime. Then you should serve a light lunch or dinner. It is also standard to serve a cake or dessert.

Music/Entertainment: For a classy touch, play soft music in the background. Sometimes, just visiting, eating, and opening gifts will take the whole time. You should have the bride provide some information to the guests about her history with the groom, or their wedding plans. It may even be a good idea to ask the groom to stop by to meet any guests he does not know. If you have a fun and slightly competitive group, you may want to play games, like Wedding Bingo or Memory (just like the real games but homemade and catered toward the bridal theme); or, guests can fill out a questionnaire about the bride and groom to see who knows the most about them. Have the bride do this as well, and consult the groom for correct answers.

While planning a party is a lot of work, the glory of hosting "the party of the year" is all yours. And that makes it all worth it!

chapter 29

The Art of Gift-Giving

How generous are you?

1. For Mother's Day last year, you:
   a. Must have missed that one . . .
   b. Sent her a card
   c. Arranged breakfast in bed, a day at the spa, and sent a dozen tulips

2. You know the birth date of:
   a. Yourself
   b. Your best friends
   c. Grandma, Grandpa, Mom, Dad, all four siblings, cousin Joe . . .

3. What are you obligated to do for your roommate on her birthday?
   a. Not lock her out
   b. Do the dishes and get a cake
   c. Arrange a surprise party for fifty close friends

If you scored:

Mostly a's: Selfishly Stingy
Mostly b's: Mindfully Mediocre
Mostly c's: Thoroughly Thoughtful

Your mom wiped your rear end for two years. Face it, you owe her one on her birthday. The handling of birthdays and other holidays varies from family to family, but I don't care where you came from—no one likes to be forgotten on the big day. You may be thinking, "But I'm a poor college student." Whah, whah, whah. I have a brother who spent $400 on a boogie board but claims he's tight on cash whenever Father's Day rolls around. It's all about sacrifice. Your parents probably ate a lot of Spaghettio's when you were born; you too can trade Pizza Hut for Chef Boyardee for a couple of days to honor your loved ones.

The most important step to becoming known as "the thoughtful child" when gift-giving is to *plan ahead*. You can pat yourself on the back for remembering your grandparents' fiftieth anniversary a day in advance, but guess what? The card still won't get there in time. The best way to handle this responsibility of adult thoughtfulness is to get organized. Grab your phone or your Microsoft Outlook, or even an old-fashioned calendar, and mark every important day that will occur over the next two semesters. Then, rewind seven days and mark a reminder the week before each event, such as "Mail card," and draw an arrow to the specified event. That gives you enough shopping and mailing time.

Which holidays do you really not want to forget? Birthdays of immediate family members should always be remembered. Your parents' wedding anniversary (if they still have one) is also an important one to recognize with at least a card. And make sure you budget for whatever special religious holidays your family celebrates with gifts (Christmas, Hanukkah, Kwanzaa, etc.). Anything you choose to celebrate with gifts beyond that is probably not expected but would surely be appreciated.

If you came from one of those families in which your dad bought Mom's Christmas present each year and signed your name to the card, you may wonder what would be considered an appropriate gift on a certain special occasion. The following is a guideline of gift-buying and sending to adhere to if you really want to be fondly missed at home. (Remember, the more missed you are, the better your chances of getting that "emergency credit card.")

For Your Parents

- *"Oh, That's Nice":* A card with a sincere note written inside, sent on time, and a phone call (don't call collect).

- *"What a Good Kid":* A semi-thoughtful, inexpensive gift and card sent on time. For example, if your dad likes to read, pick out the latest best-seller. Moms usually like a pair of earrings or something from Bath and Body Works.

- *"That's Our Golden Child":* If you have not already achieved this level of familial stardom, it's not too late. In fact, a parent's heart grows much fonder of your memory after you leave. A good gift just guarantees the title. The Golden Child will begin shopping for a special occasion at least two weeks in advance, probably without a reminder from a handheld device. He will arrange golf lessons for Pops, courtesy of his old, high school buddy at the pro shop. Or, he'll buy a hat or sweatshirt from the bookstore with the proud words "(fill in the blank) State University Dad." For Mom, she'll place a sentimental picture of herself and mother in a "miss you" frame, and/or call 1-800-FLOWERS to send a bouquet. Another surefire golden gift for Mom is anything inscribed or fluffy and in the color of the living room. The most important key to the Golden Child's gift is the card, which will include a heart-felt message of at least ten sentences. Yes, ten. Possible included phrases will be: "I never knew how good I had it before I left home"; "There's nothing I miss more than your chocolate-chip pancakes"; and "You are my hero." Start the day with an early morning phone call home and the words, "I just wanted to be the first one to wish you a Happy Birthday!"

For Your Siblings

- *"I'm so glad you left and I got your room"*: If your little sister said this when you left home, chances are you don't even know how old she is, let alone the date of her birth. Surprise her. Call her on the appropriate day and sincerely wish her a good one. To really shock her, also send a card. It's okay if it's late—she would expect nothing more.

- *"I would never touch your TV, drive your car, borrow your sweater"*: If you do have a good, respectful relationship with your siblings, it will only improve with a remembered holiday. For younger children, have fun visiting a toy store and relive your childhood. For them, toys are always better than clothes. For teenagers, iTunes gift cards usually go over well. And the no-risk gifts that everyone appreciates are gift certificates to favorite stores or magazine subscriptions. (This also saves money on postage.)

For Your Grandparents and Other Somewhat Close Relatives

- *"Which one are you again?"* Whether you are from a really big family or you just don't see your relatives all that much, they are probably not expecting much from you on Christmas. Honestly, just a phone call would be nice.

- *"What a chip off the old block!"* On the other hand, grandparents can really come in handy. They can enlarge your cheering section at graduation and send you homemade snickerdoodles during finals. Return the favor. If you have grandparents, remember their birthdays and anniversaries. You don't necessarily have to spend any money. I promise you there is nothing they would want more than a letter and a picture of their favorite grandchild.

For Your Old High School Friends

Your friends are most likely not going to expect gifts from you. You're all in the same boat, and they'll understand your financial situation. In fact, you will be making new friends each day in your new environment. But, don't let that ruin the relationships you left behind. There's nothing better than reliving high school memories during Christmas vacation. But while away at school or working away from home, keep in touch. Phone, write, or—hello, cyber friends—email! It's probably free!

Don't Forget the Thank Yous!

Remember how you got that stationery as a graduation gift that had the words "Thank You" scrolled all over it? There's actually something you are supposed to do with that. You see, for the special occasions in *your* life, people will be sending you gifts! But, if you want to make sure you receive gifts from those people next year, you'd better learn how to write a thank you note.

Even if your parents didn't make you send thank you notes, it is still something you should do to show your gratitude for other people's thoughtfulness, even if the purple boxers Grandma sent you will surely not be worn. For those of you who groan at the thought of actually completing an act of written correspondence, rest assured. Thank you notes are much easier to write than letters. They only need to be a few sentences long; and if you're not sure what to say, you can follow this simple formula:

1. Address the gift giver with the phrase "Dear ___."
2. (Sentence) Thank the person for the specific gift he/she sent.
3. (Sentence) Tell how you can use the gift, or why you appreciate it.
4. (Sentence) Mention how thoughtful the person is for sending the gift.
5. Close with the word "Sincerely," or "Love," and your name.

Here's an example:

Dear Grandma,

Thank you so much for the purple boxers! I will surely wear them daily, and the color makes me feel so manly. It was so thoughtful of you to send such a useful gift for my birthday. Looking forward to seeing you soon!

Love,

Johnnyboy

Always send a thank you note, even if you don't find the gift sent to you particularly useful. Thank you notes assure the sender you received the present, make them feel great for sending the gift, and almost guarantee that you will receive a gift next year, even if it's just another pair of purple boxers.

chapter 30

How full is your life?

1. Your motto in life is:
    a. Stop and smell the roses
    b. Every rose has its thorn
    c. All roses die

2. Your cup is:
    a. Half full
    b. Half empty
    c. Shattered

3. The last thing you said to someone was:
    a. "Have a great day!"
    b. "Whatever!"
    c. "It's not fair..."

If you scored:
Mostly a's: Life of the party!
Mostly b's: Just living . . .
Mostly c's: Life stinks!

Are you truly living every moment of your life to its fullest, or is your mere existence a waste of oxygen? Despite your moral and religious preferences, there is a code of goodness that is granted upon most people by nature or nurture. This desire to perpetuate goodness is what gives people the determination needed to make earth a better place. Even though nobody's perfect, credit is deserved by those who strive to be better. Here are ten lessons in life that the common man ignores. But if followed, they will ensure that you exceed normalcy and become a truly great person.

1 **Be 100 percent responsible for your life.** "It's not my fault" is said much more than, "I'm sorry" and "How can we fix this?" But, if you want to be in control of your own life, never blame incidents that affect you on someone else—even if they're not your fault. This creates a stubborn attitude that results in a prideful person. Aren't you the Master of Your Own Destiny? While fate is powerful, you are in control of how it affects your life.

Now, I'm not suggesting that you run around and tell everyone how sorry you are all the time. Instead, be proactive and preventive. If you are driving in front of a reckless hooligan who appears to be DUI, don't just pull over and let him pass. Call the police and make sure he gets stopped, before someone else gets hurt. If you wind up in a bad marriage, don't say, "Oh well, I must have fallen out of love." Instead think, "I choose to love this person, so I'm going to make it work." If someone at work did something that is going to make your boss or your company look bad, don't just think, "Oh well, not my problem." Confront the person and do what you can to fix the problem before it hits the roof. Get out and vote—yes, your vote counts (as Florida is well aware). Pick up the cans littering your yard—even if they're not yours. An attitude of obliviousness destroys great possibilities. So, take responsibility.

2 **"Whether you think you can or think you can't, you're right!" —Henry Ford.** Your attitude is the central factor to your success in life. Have conviction in whatever you do, and if you're graced with a little luck and put in a lot of hard work, in most cases, it will happen! Think of all the proactive dreamers who have changed our world because they believed in their cause: George Washington, Susan B. Anthony, Martin Luther King, Jr., the Wright Brothers, Mother Theresa, philosophers, firefighters, teachers, and artists. Idealistic people who turn their thoughts into actions get things done.

Someone once criticized me by saying that I act like I can do anything. Well in my humble opinion, *why not?* There is no reason to limit yourself by what the world thinks is "normal" or "doable." With the right attitude, you can truly do anything you want!

3 **Obey both legal and moral laws.** Before you do any questionable act, ask yourself, "Is it legal?" Then more importantly, ask yourself, "Is it moral?" The r easons for obeying the laws of the government are obvious—you don't want to be arrested, you don't want to go to jail, you don't want a record . . . But the reasoning behind moral laws isn't as obvious to some people. While you probably won't get arrested for not having a high moral code, it will not fare you well in life. Instead, you should want to protect people and make the world a better place. For example:

Legal: You shouldn't speed because you'll get a ticket; Moral: You shouldn't drive while you are tired because you could fall asleep at the wheel and hurt somebody. Legal: You shouldn't abuse your girlfriend; Moral: You shouldn't cheat on your girlfriend because that makes you dishonest and not trustworthy. Legal: You shouldn't steal from people; Moral: You shouldn't take advantage of people and con them out of their money. Realize that moral laws are just as important as the legal ones, even if they are not inscribed at City Hall.

4 **Believe that money does not buy happiness.** It is okay to want enough money to live comfortably and to help other people and causes, but money should never be more important to you than your loved ones or your values. Sure, you just want to drive your dream car, but once you can afford it, then you'll want a nicer house and garage to go with it. And your nicer house will need a bigger yard, and your yard will need a swimming pool, and you'll love the water so much you'll want a boat, and then a vacation house to go with that. It never stops! Even wealthy people get into debt, and just want more, because the lust after money is a dangerous cycle. If you don't believe me, go ask the former NBA players and rock stars who now work at car washes.

Money does not buy happiness; but it does buy pride and selfishness. The literary genius C.S. Lewis said, "Pride gets no pleasure out of having something, only out of having more of it than the next man." Would you even care what designer label was in your shoes, if no one else ever saw you wear them? I remember being a proud little girl and calling up my best friend when I was in the second grade to rattle off all of the Christmas presents Santa had brought me, just crossing my fingers that my list was better or longer than hers. Since then, I have been more fully exposed to the world and some of the conditions people live in, and I am almost ashamed at all I have compared to many perfectly innocent, homeless children. Why spend $30 million dollars on a house when you could feed 3,000 starving children for a year, instead?

5 **Think before you judge.** Have you ever silently—or not so silently—cursed at that little old man driving 10 miles under the speed limit for slowing you down? I know I used to all the time, until someone once pointed out to me that the little old man might be on his way home from his wife's funeral, her death resulting from a car accident in which she was hit by someone who was speeding. That changed my perspective! Sure, you may be in a hurry to go somewhere

important to you, but there is certainly someone out there who is struggling in a worse way.

We need to cut people a little slack, because everyone else is just as important as we are, and we never know what another person is going through. The next time a crying newborn in a movie theatre annoys you until it is taken out, just be glad you're not the baby's mother who probably gets three hours of sleep a night, and who is just dying to get out of the house, but can't afford a babysitter and a movie. The next time your food comes out late, don't complain to a waitress who has probably been working two shifts with a short-handed, incompetent kitchen staff. Have a little patience with people, instead of immediately jumping on the judgmental bandwagon.

6 **Forget yourself!** "Poor me, life sucks, I've got it so rough, whaaah." Stop complaining! No matter who you are, there is someone who has it worse. Even if your life is pretty rough, at least you can read—there are millions who are illiterate! Whenever you start to pity your life, get off the couch and go help someone who really does have it worse.

A close friend of mine recently went through a long and painful divorce. One time when I asked her how she was doing, she said, "You know, I was making a list of all the things that could be worse and there are a lot of them—I could have been in a concentration camp, I could have to watch a child die, I could have a horrible disease where my skin deteriorates. I don't have it that bad." Next time you are feeling sorry for yourself, go feed the homeless or visit a children's hospital for a little perspective, and be grateful for what you have!

7 **You can't change others—you can only change yourself.** This is a secret that could save so many relationships, if people only believed it was true. When you are going through a difficult experience with someone, realize that you can't choose the other person's actions; you can only control your

reactions. We really can't understand what someone else is thinking in a situation because our paradigms are so different, so it's pointless to try to get people to act and react the way we do.

If you are in a close relationship with someone who is abusive—whether verbally or physically, do not expect that person to change. Although hopefully some day he or she will, you are not in power of that decision. The only thing you can do about it is to leave the relationship. Likewise, if someone annoys you in a menial way, you probably cannot stop that person from being a slob, belching uncontrollably, or criticizing everything you do. Instead, change your reactions to their behavior, no matter how inappropriate it is. Or, just avoid that person altogether. That way you are not allowing your own mood to be affected.

8 **"It's not how far you fall, but how high you bounce."** **(author unknown)** Life is about overcoming challenges and learning from them. It would be boring if nothing ever went wrong, because then we would never appreciate how good we have it the rest of the time. When you find yourself going through a rough time, try to learn from it, so that when you hit bottom, you can "bounce" even higher and become a better person than you were before.

Your background or the projected sociological statistics for your future should not determine what you become. Another unknown author said, "What lies behind you and what lies before you are insignificant to what lies within you." Even if you are poor and uneducated, you can rise above that and beat the odds, like so many other awe-inspiring people.

9 **Don't take life for granted!** Remember the last time you had the flu and were throwing up all day and suffering the aches and pains and a horrible headache? Did you happen to think (as I always do), "As soon as I get over this, I'm really going to appreciate my health!" Well, don't wait until you get sick to appreciate the health you once had. Enjoy it now!

If you are fortunate enough to be educated, have a good family, look somewhat attractive, and have enough dough to pay the bills, be grateful each and every day! Once a loved one dies, it is too late for "quality time." If you get in an accident and become paralyzed, it is too late to walk along the beach. Once you have kids and become financially drained, it isn't as convenient to travel the world. Take advantage of every opportunity now, and appreciate that you can! Don't live the rest of your life dwelling on what might have been.

10 "This above all: to thine own self be true," **William Shakespeare, Hamlet.** Live your life for *you*. Don't let your parents, your peers, or your professors tell you what your destiny is. Prove them wrong; beat the odds. Follow your instincts and create your own happiness. You will never be able to earn enough money to make a job you hate worthwhile. You will never get over your lost true love, even if he or she wasn't "good enough" for your family. You will never develop true strength of character if you are too scared to stand against the crowd on a moral issue you deeply support. Be true to yourself.

When I was in high school, I wasn't a regular fixture with the "in" crowd. While in ninth grade, I lost my best friend of three years to the wily ways of popularity. I wasn't a partier, and therefore she deemed me unworthy to hang with her crowd because I was "different." The next few years were lonely and awkward as I struggled to make friends and find my place in other hallways of high school. I learned an important lesson, though. It seemed that the popular crowd was a small group who thought they were *it*. But actually, a rather large crowd lingered on the outside, and in that group, there were lots of friends to be made and people to get to know. There, I found many friends who would allow me to be me.

While most of my friends did go to the parties, I spent many weekend nights babysitting or, ouch, doing homework.

But I was nice to everyone, and as time went on, I met more and more people on the outskirts through organizations like student government, drama, volleyball, and church. I was never "popular," but I was happy.

By some shocking twist of fate, during my senior year, I was elected my high school's Homecoming Queen. On the night I was crowned, a girl who I had always admired came up to me and said, "You know the reason you won? Because people respect you." I learned that for me in high school, I would rather be respected than popular. And you know what? In the Real World, maintaining your self-respect is the most important key to survival.

Acknowledgments

This book would have been impossible without the inspiration of all the clueless, eighteen-year-old know-it-alls (including myself) who once left home expecting to conquer the world—until they realized they were unsure how to unload the dishwasher. I especially thank those siblings in particular whose late-night calls inspired many of the anecdotes in this book.

I am much obliged to Karen Kirkwood, Cecelia Knox, Kathy Jones, Paula Harline, Louise Plummer, and Chris Crowe—who instilled in me the passion to write. And to Anne Lamott, Martha Fuller, Barbara Potter, my book club, and my writer's group, who have further stoked the fire.

Thanks to Claire Gerus for first bringing this book to life—here's to many more rounds! And much, much appreciation to my dear friend Amy Cook, who has prodded me along, produced this edition, and who never ceases to amaze me.

Much appreciation to my parents and grandparents—and in particular my mom, who taught me that "the greatest thing a parent can do for a child is to teach her independence." You did well.

This book is dedicated to my four love monkeys, who may need it someday if I don't do my job. Thanks for being patient when Mommy hides behind her screen. And as always, thanks to Michael—my best friend, favorite editor, and the greatest husband ever. I love you with all my heart.